Houghton
Mifflin
Harcourt

On Our Way to English®

Student Edition

ON YOUR WAY

You're on your way to English. Soon you will listen, speak, read, and write English as if you had been doing it your whole life! This book will get you there, and so will your teacher.

Be yourself. Tell others what you think about what you are learning. Invite them to share their thoughts with you, too.

Sometimes your classmates will help you. Sometimes you'll help them. Even though you come from different places, you are all on the same journey.

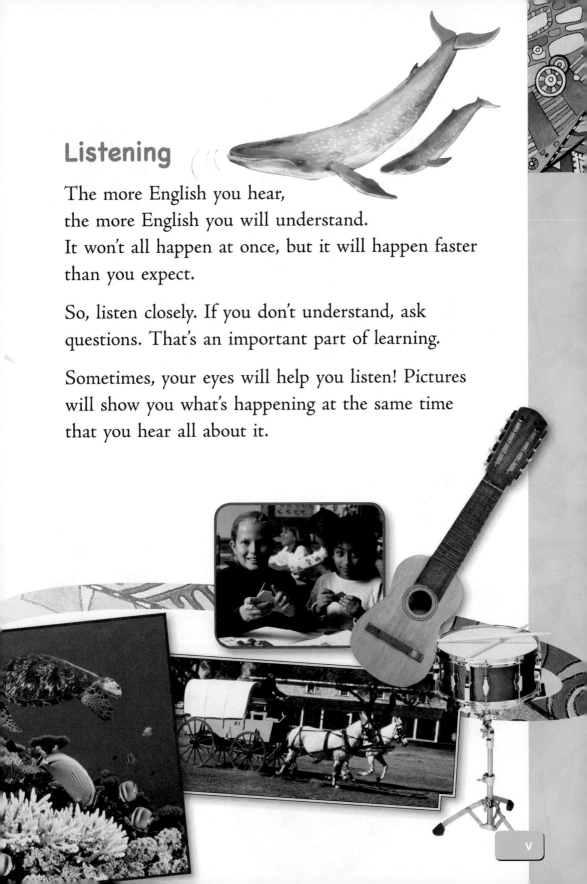

Listening

The more English you hear,
the more English you will understand.
It won't all happen at once, but it will happen faster
than you expect.

So, listen closely. If you don't understand, ask
questions. That's an important part of learning.

Sometimes, your eyes will help you listen! Pictures
will show you what's happening at the same time
that you hear all about it.

Speaking

With this program, you'll learn and say new English words every day. You'll learn how to put the words together. Your English will get better and better.

Speaking English will help you in almost every part of your life. You'll be able to share information and ideas. You'll be able to express your own thoughts and opinions in English.

Reading

Most of the words you will see in the United States are written in English. You can see words everywhere. They tell you the news. They give you the information you need. They tell you stories, and they tell you what people are like all around the world. Without words, you'd miss out on almost everything!

In this book, you will learn how to understand simple ideas that are written down. Then you'll start to understand written ideas that aren't so simple. Keep going, and you'll get there.

Writing

You'll listen to English, speak it, and read it, too. As you do, you'll learn more words and more ways to put them together. At the same time, you'll be using what you learn to write in English.

You'll learn about different kinds of writing. You'll write your own letters, stories, and reports in English. Your teacher will show you how to start each writing project. Then you'll learn how to improve your work and make it really great!

GET GOING

The most important piece of the puzzle is you. You'll know when you're doing well and when you need help. It will be your job to push yourself ahead.

Keep going. You're on your way to English.

Contents

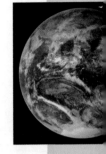

Road to Freedom

The BIG Question

What is freedom?

☐ What are some reasons people leave their homelands?

☐ Why did the American colonists fight for their freedom?

☐ Does freedom mean the same thing to everybody?

Let's Talk

What causes are important to people?

1. Why is liberty important to people?

People who are free are able to…

- ☐ choose their own leaders.
- ☐ decide what jobs they will do.
- ☐ have equal rights and equal treatment.
- ☐ speak out about what they believe.

2. How can people disagree peacefully about important ideas?

People can disagree by…

- ☐ writing to a newspaper.
- ☐ protesting in a group.
- ☐ speaking out in public.
- ☐ working to change the laws.

3. **How do people defend their freedom?**

   To defend their freedom, people...

   ☐ fight battles.

   ☐ leave their homeland.

   ☐ risk their lives.

   ☐ get others to join
   with them.

4. **How can we honor people who have tried to make our country better?**

   We can...

   ☐ remember people who did
   great deeds in the past.

   ☐ learn about battles, marches,
   and other events.

   ☐ tell others about
   what happened.

   ☐ see what we can do to
   make things even better.

Say **more!**

British
colony
protest
Boston Tea Party
declare
independence
march
liberty

Theme Vocabulary

The easiest way to remember the meaning of a new word is to use it. As you discuss the Revolutionary War, use these vocabulary words. Use them when you read and write about the Revolutionary War, too.

Read the word.
Look at the picture.
Use the word in a sentence.

British

colony

protest

Boston Tea Party

declare

independence

march

liberty

Which Picture?

Look at the vocabulary cards. Choose one picture. Don't tell anyone what it is! Describe the picture. See if your partner can guess which picture you chose.

Good Advice

Mr. Fred   Michael   Randall

1

Mr. Fred, I need your help with a little problem I have.

Why me? I've got problems of my own.

But you've been around. You know a lot, Mr. Fred.

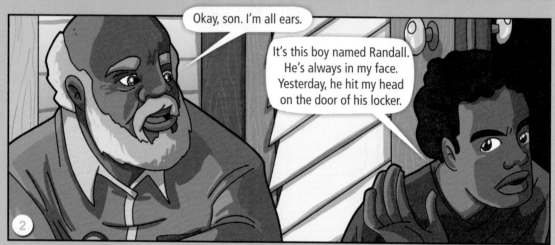

2

Okay, son. I'm all ears.

It's this boy named Randall. He's always in my face. Yesterday, he hit my head on the door of his locker.

3

Looks like you're doing a bang-up job, Dude.

Ow!

7 **Formal/Informal Language** When someone "gets into hot water," they get into trouble. Is this formal language or informal language?

10 Expressions When we say that finding something is "like looking for a needle in a haystack," we mean that the thing is "almost impossible to find."

The 13 British Colonies

A **colony** is a group of people that have left their native land to live in a new land. The government of the native land rules the colony. By 1733, thirteen colonies in North America belonged to Britain. A king ruled Britain. The king and his government ruled the colonies.

NORTH
AMERICA

N
W   E
S

SOUTH
AMERICA

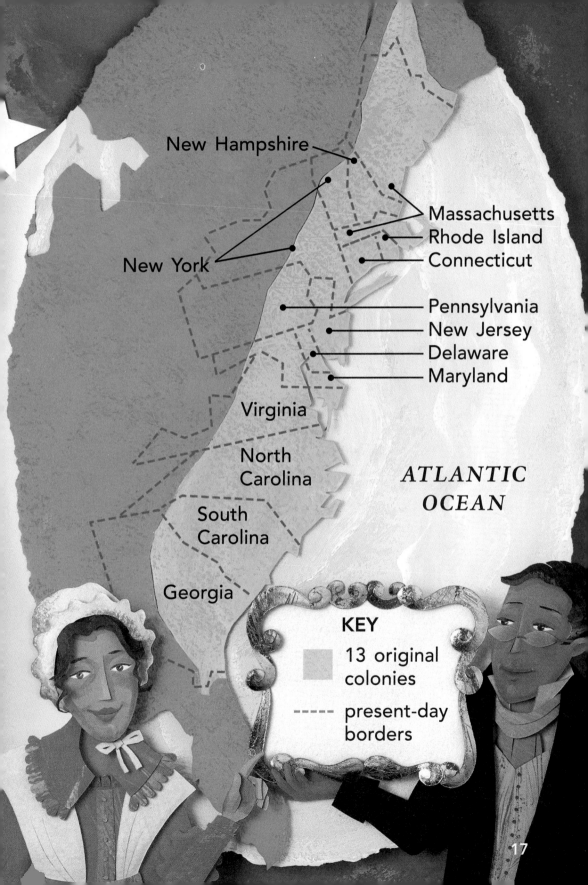

New Hampshire

Massachusetts

Rhode Island

Connecticut

New York

Pennsylvania

New Jersey

Delaware

Maryland

Virginia

North Carolina

ATLANTIC OCEAN

South Carolina

Georgia

KEY

13 original colonies

----- present-day borders

17

The Harvest

by Duncan Sharp

Matt Van Pelt sharpened his scythe. His crop of wheat was finally ready. "There will be enough to pay Landlord Schuyler his rent," Matt told himself, "as long as the **British** don't come."

The British were coming, though. Just north of Matt's fields, Private Billy Harker helped push cannons across a muddy stream. "I'm starving," Billy muttered. He couldn't wait to reach the rebels' fertile farmlands. There would be wheat to make bread then.

Lady Catherine Schuyler was headed to the farmlands, too. Her family owned most of it. "Faster," she called to her coachman. "The British army must not get any of the grain!"

At Matt's farm, the coach rolled to a stop. "Matthias Van Pelt," Lady Schuyler called. "Your country needs you."

Matt listened to Lady Schuyler. "What you ask cannot be right," he finally said.

"For a patriot," she replied, "it is right. Without our grain, the British army cannot feed themselves or fight."

A light breeze rustled the wheat. Matt bent low and touched a torch to his crop. Wind swept the flames, and the fields burned red. Matt stood back and watched the harvest— a harvest of freedom.

The American Revolution:
1775 – 1783
by Rita Yee

By 1767, the people in the American colonies were angry. The British were taxing them for many things. These things included sugar, tea, and paint. The colonists had not had a representative in the British government when the tax laws were passed. Many colonists felt that this was unfair.

The colonists complained. To **protest** the law, many people stopped buying British goods. Instead, they bought supplies from other countries. This was against British law. In 1768, the British sent an army to North America to restore order.

Tension Builds

In 1773, several British ships sailed into Boston harbor. The ships were loaded with tea. The colonists did not want to pay the tax on the tea. They demanded that the ships return to England. But the ships remained.

Then one night, about sixty colonists boarded one of the British ships. The men threw over three hundred chests filled with tea into the harbor. This famous act of protest is now known as the **Boston Tea Party**.

The British decided to punish the colonies for the loss of the expensive tea. The British army closed the Boston port. Another new law made town meetings illegal.

The War Begins

In 1774, chosen representatives from the colonies met in Philadelphia. The group was called the First Continental Congress. They met to discuss what to do about Britain and the new laws. However, this action did not force Britain to change the laws.

Tension between Britain and the colonies grew worse. Britain sent more **troops** to North America. The colonists began arming themselves. They also practiced how to fight in **battle**.

On the night of April 19, 1775, British soldiers **marched** to Concord, a small town in Massachusetts. They had been ordered to search for guns and ammunition. A colonist named Paul Revere and some other men rode on horseback

ahead of the soldiers to warn the colonists. The colonists armed themselves and prepared for the worst.

The next day the colonists and the British army clashed in the Battles of Lexington and Concord. The fighting of the American **Revolution** had truly begun.

The Second Continental Congress

A Second Continental Congress met in May in Philadelphia. It created the Continental Army. It chose George Washington as leader. Washington and his army acted quickly. They forced the British army out of Boston.

The Continental Congress argued about a key issue. Some members wanted the colonies to **declare** their **independence** from Britain and become a new nation. Others didn't want to declare anything. They still thought of themselves as British.

A committee was formed to write a Declaration of Independence from England. It decided that one person should draft the **document**. The other members would make changes later. The members chose Thomas Jefferson to write

the draft. The document would state the colonists' reasons for breaking away from Great Britain.

Not long after, the Declaration of Independence was approved. The date was July 4, 1776. It is an important date in history. It marks the beginning of a new nation, the United States of America.

Battles and Victory

Fighting continued throughout the colonies. In October 1777, the British lost the Battle of Saratoga, in New York. The tide of the war was changing. Countries around the world began to think that the Americans could win. France sent arms and other aid.

In 1781, a final battle at Yorktown, Virginia, ended the war. The Americans had won their **liberty**! In 1783, the British signed a treaty recognizing the United States as an independent nation.

Prove It

What things did the Continental Congress do to help gain American independence? What evidence did you use?

They Came to Help

by Nick Skouras

Many people in Europe believed in the colonists' cause. Two men who did were Tadeusz Kosciuszko (tah-day-OOSH kosh-YOOS-koe) and the Marquis de Lafayette (mar-KEE dih lah-fie-ETTE).

The Engineer from Poland

Kosciuszko was born in Poland. In 1776, he crossed the Atlantic to join the colonists' fight for freedom. Kosciuszko was made a colonel in the Continental Army. He worked as an engineer. An engineer plans and builds structures. His main duties were to plan how to defend towns against attack, to build forts, and to decide where to place cannons. His first job was to make the city of Philadelphia safe against British attack.

Kosciuszko later planned the defense of Albany, in northern New York. He built defenses in the nearby forests and hills.

In October 1777, the Battle of Saratoga took place in that area. The Americans were able to surround the British. Kosciuszko had helped the colonists win a major battle.

Later he worked in other regions. His efforts and his bravery in battle helped the Americans win the war.

The Nobleman from France

In 1777, the Marquis de Lafayette sailed from his home in France to the United States. He was just nineteen. He was, however, a rich nobleman and an experienced soldier.

He arrived in his own ship and with a lot of money. He offered to help the Americans. They accepted, and Lafayette was made a general. This turned out to be a wise move.

Lafayette fought bravely in many battles. He also gave the Americans money to buy supplies for their troops.

In 1779, Lafayette helped to convince the French government to send troops to join the colonists' cause. In 1781, Lafayette and the French troops played an important part in the final stage of the war. They helped surround the British army so that it could not escape. The British were forced to surrender at Yorktown, Virginia, ending the war.

from Early THUNDER

by Jean Fritz

In stories about the American Revolution, it often seems that everyone in the Colonies supported independence. In fact, between 1/5 and 1/3 of colonists were loyal to England. These Loyalists, or Tories, believed that problems with the English government could be settled peacefully. The Patriots, or Whigs, wanted to break away from England.

Daniel West's Loyalist father is the town doctor in Salem, Massachusetts. The year is 1774. Both Whigs and Tories are angry at the tax on English tea. In protest, people are **refusing** to buy or drink tea. However, Judge Ropes, a neighbor, is very sick with smallpox. This is a contagious disease that killed many people in those days. Judge Ropes has asked for tea, which makes him feel better. Daniel and his friend Beckett look everywhere for tea. They finally go to the spare room, a cold room to store food safely in the winter.

People are very frightened of smallpox. They think that cats and dogs spread the disease. A law was passed in Salem that no one could keep a dog or cat.

"If there is any tea," he said at last, "this is a likely place."

One by one, Daniel and Beckett took the lids off the crocks. They smelled. Apple butter. Mincemeat. Sage. Fennel. There was no tea.

"Sorry," Daniel said. "I guess not."

Beckett sat down on the edge of the bed. He was working his hands again. "Daniel," he said. "Folks are mad at the Judge. Because he doesn't go to the Pest House. Daniel, he's too sick to go anywhere."

"Who's mad?"

"Liberty people. I heard the talk in town. They're just looking to fault him because he's a Tory. They claim he wants to get back at them for insisting he go against the new law and take his salary from the province instead of the crown. Daniel—"

"Yes?"

"They say he *wants* to spread the smallpox."

Daniel groaned. "After all the Judge has done for Salem, people can say that!"

"They can say anything. They can say the Judge has deliberately loosed his cat into the streets."

"The Judge never had a cat."

"I know."

"Oh, Beckett, let's think." Daniel cast about in his mind for friends who might have hidden some tea. Someone they could go to at this time of night.

"What about that trunk?" Beckett asked, pointing to the wall. "Any hope of some being hidden there?"

Daniel held out no hope but he moved the four plum puddings that were on the lid and he opened it. Just as he thought, the trunk was filled with folded materials—lengths of dress goods, summer quilts, extra sheets, shirting. Daniel thrust his hand down one side and struck something hard. He pushed aside the cloth and pulled out a large tin box. There was no marking on it. He pried off the lid and he smiled at Beckett. There was no mistaking the odor of tea. They held the tin up to their noses and breathed deeply.

"Ah-h," Beckett sighed. "I'd forgotten." He took another deep breath. "Do you suppose, Daniel . . . sometime . . . ?"

He didn't need to finish the sentence. Daniel grinned. "Maybe," he said. "Sometime."

While Beckett was sniffing, Daniel found an empty jar and filled it from the tin. "You know, Beckett," he said, "I'm glad of one thing. Folks can't visit a person with smallpox. No one can tell Judge Ropes what's being said about him. At least while he's sick, he won't know."

The two boys went out of the room but at the door to his bedroom Daniel stopped. "You wait for me in the kitchen," he said. "I'm going to put on my clothes and come along."

There wasn't apt to be *real* danger, Daniel told himself, shivering in the cold room as he got dressed. The Liberty Boys had done some pretty ornery things but so far nothing that would actually hurt a person. Still, he and Beckett would be no match for them and when they went out, it would be best not to meet anyone. Instead of walking in the middle of the street, the way a person normally would, they would stick to the shadows.

Zoom In

How did Beckett and Daniel know that there was tea inside the tin box? What evidence is in the story?

But as soon as Daniel and Beckett stepped out the back door, these plans were forgotten. The town was no longer quiet. The boys ran around the corner of the house to the main street, the part that was called Paved Street because it was the only street in town that was paved. To the right in the next block where Beckett and Judge Ropes lived lanterns were moving around. They didn't seem to be going anyplace— just back and forth, up and down. To the left there was nothing to see, only to hear. From the direction of the Common came the sound of singing. Daniel couldn't quite catch the words but he knew what they'd be. From the Liberty Song:

> "Our right arms are ready,
> Steady, men, steady!"

It was the Whigs celebrating the repeal of the stamp tax, acting as if it were *their* holiday, as if only *they* had a right to mark it.

Daniel and Beckett took to the middle of the road and ran to the right toward the lanterns. Ten or fifteen people were in front of Judge Ropes' house. They had coats on over nightclothes. Men had their bare feet thrust into boots; few had even taken time to put on hats. As Daniel and Beckett ran up, no one spoke. Mr. Foote, Beckett's father, simply pointed to Judge Ropes' house. It was dark except for a light in the kitchen on the right side. It took Daniel a minute to see what was wrong. Then he drew in his breath. Every window in the front of Judge Ropes' house was broken. Mr. Foote stepped closer and held up his lantern. Glass was strewn all over the lawn. Along with the glass were rocks and bricks; the rest, Daniel figured, were in the house.

Zoom In

What do Daniel and Beckett discover when they arrive at Judge Ropes' house? What part of the story describes this?

Mr. Foote tried to describe what had happened but all that came out was how quick it had been. A gang evidently had crept up quietly, let loose all at once with the bricks and rocks they had come armed with, and by the time the neighbors were outside, they'd pounded off. It had all taken place, Daniel guessed, while he and Beckett were in the pie room.

"Didn't anyone go after them?" Daniel cried.

Mr. Foote nodded. "Yes. Nathaniel, the Judge's son. And some others. But they won't find them. By now they're all part of the big crowd celebrating on the Common."

Daniel looked around at the people standing on the street—neighbors, Whigs and Tories together, helpless, angry. Some of the women were crying; the men were pacing, talking in short shocked sentences.

Beckett stepped near the house. "Miranda!" he called. His voice didn't come out very loud but even so Daniel winced. It was as if the night itself had somehow been hurt and any sound, no matter what kind, was more than it could stand. Beckett waited a moment, then called louder. "Miranda! Come on out here. Daniel West has something for the Judge."

Slowly the kitchen door opened. At first there was just a square of light on the steps; then Miranda stepped out into the light, holding a lantern over her head and squinting nearsightedly at the street. Like everyone else, her clothes were in disarray and she wasn't wearing her mobcap. Her shoulders sagging, she obviously didn't know or care that under the lantern folks could see that she was all but bald.

"They've gone, Miranda," Beckett said gently. "It's all right. We're all friends here." Daniel set the jar down in the middle of the street, then everyone backed up while Miranda walked slowly out from the house. It was the only way a person could send something into a smallpox house without spreading the disease. The line of onlookers, backed up as far as they could, stood quietly and respectfully as Miranda approached the jar.

As she bent down, Mrs. Foote spoke. "Tell the Judge, Miranda, that the damage was done by a few ruffians. Tell him the town loves him."

Miranda straightened up. "I did tell him that, Mrs. Foote."

"What did he say?"

"He didn't say anything. His heart is broken."

Miranda made her way back into the house. No one moved until the kitchen door closed.

Then Captain Pickering spoke. He was one of the town's leading Whigs and a good friend of the Judge.

"What was in that jar?" he asked.

Daniel was standing on the edge of the group. He whirled around.

"Tea!" he shouted. "It was a blasted jar of English tea!"

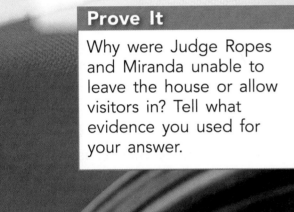

Prove It

Why were Judge Ropes and Miranda unable to leave the house or allow visitors in? Tell what evidence you used for your answer.

A WARNING IN COAL

by Barbara Mather

Chapter 1

The April sun warmed Jim as he walked along Common Street. It was late in the morning. He had just helped his father deliver bundles of paper to Mr. Thomas. Jim knew that Mr. Thomas was printing a new **pamphlet** to distribute. His father had told him that many patriots explained their cause in newspaper articles and pamphlets.

As he turned a corner, Jim saw a group of British soldiers march towards him. The soldiers always made him nervous. Jim was always a little afraid that they would see his secrets written on his face. Jim's father was a member of the group calling themselves the Sons of Liberty. The winter before last, Father had been one of the men who boarded the British ship and dumped the chests of tea overboard. This act had enraged the British. They were always looking for the men who had taken part in the Boston Tea Party.

Jim knew even more. He had overheard his father talking about the group's leader, Samuel Adams. He had heard some other names, too. But Jim, like his father, believed in the patriots' cause. He knew that these were secrets that people who supported the British did not need to know. He had never told anyone what he knew.

As Jim walked by the soldiers, one pointed to him. "Come here, lad," the soldier said.

Jim froze in his tracks. But how could he refuse a request from an armed British soldier? He came forward.

For a moment, the man looked Jim over as if trying to read his mind. Jim kept his expression as blank as he could.

"My, my," said another of the soldiers. "You've scared the lad to death." With that the group passed by, still laughing.

"That was a mean trick," a voice behind Jim said. Jim turned. There stood a girl he recognized. He had met her very briefly two days ago. He had delivered some fine stationery to her house. She was several years older than Jim and very pretty. She gave him a little smile.

"Dorothy! Don't speak to strangers," scolded the woman walking with her.

"He's not a stranger, Mother. He's the boy who delivered my stationery," the girl said.

"He could still be a rebel," said the woman sternly. "Come along."

Jim knew that only colonists who supported the king used the word *rebel*. He would never have called his father a rebel. Father and his friends were patriots. They wanted to protect the rights of colonists.

Jim didn't know much about the girl and the woman except that they were probably loyal to the British king. He didn't bother to argue his side. He only bowed politely to them, and they nodded back to him. Jim let them walk on ahead of him.

The street was crowded with people on foot and on horseback. Some distance away, Jim could still see the group of British soldiers. Their red-coated uniforms stood out in the sunlight. The rest of the people were of all ages, all sizes, wearing all kinds of clothing, from rich to ragged.

Of course Jim could easily tell which side the soldiers were on, but was it possible to tell about anyone else? Being rich or poor didn't seem to be the way to judge. One of the city's fiercest patriots, John Hancock, was one of its richest men.

After picking up a packet of paper, Jim went to Mr. Webster's shop to order ink. As Jim was leaving, Mr. Webster said, "I wonder if you could take a message to your father."

Jim had a sudden urge to refuse the request. What if this action put him in danger? But he nodded his head. He was old enough to help the cause.

There was no one else in the shop, but anyone could look into the window. Mr. Webster turned away, so that his actions would not look suspicious to a passer-by. Then he whispered, "Sam Adams is hiding in Concord."

Zoom In

What details show you that everyone in Boston doesn't feel the same way about Britain?

Jim tried to look casual as he walked home. He had to deliver Mr. Webster's message quickly. Father would need to relay the news to other people. With all the soldiers around, the Sons of Liberty might need to protect Mr. Adams. It would be terrible if he were captured by the British.

As Jim approached his father's shop, he saw some red-coated British soldiers at the front door. Jim ducked behind a barrel on the street.

Chapter 2

Jim backed into the alley to get out of the soldiers' sight. What were soldiers doing in his father's printing shop? Were they just checking buildings at will? Had they received information about Father? *Was Father in danger?*

And how was Jim going to relay Mr. Webster's information with soldiers standing right there?

Suddenly, Jim noticed a small chunk of coal in the dirt beside him. He glanced at the blank pages under his arm. A plan sprang into his head.

A few minutes later, Jim walked calmly across the street and past the British soldiers. "Hello, gentlemen," he said. "I have a delivery of paper for this printer."

"Go on, boy," one soldier said. "And don't bother us. But wait. Let me see the paper." Jim held out the sheaf of paper. It was tied up with string. The man riffled the corners rapidly to give the pages a quick look. "All right," he said. "It's just a pile of blank paper for the printer."

When Jim entered the shop, he saw his father sitting on a stool surrounded by more British soldiers. "Good day, Mr. Crawford," said Jim. "I'm here to deliver the paper you ordered. Now I'll be on my way home."

Jim looked respectfully at his father. Father played along and did not show any expression. Jim walked out of the shop and saluted the soldiers. Then he crossed the street and turned into the alley. He stopped and peeked around the corner of the building at his father's shop. He waited for the soldiers to march away to the end of the street and turn the corner. Then he returned to the shop.

Once inside, he saw that the string was off the packet of paper. Father picked Jim up and hugged him. "That's was quite some trick," said Father. "Hiding your message in the middle of the blank pages. I have to run now and tell some other friends the news. We all need to be ready for whatever happens next. I'll be back in an hour," he added. "If all goes well, you will grow up in a different world from this one."

Prove It

In what ways is Jim like his father? Use evidence from the story for your answer.

pamphlet
refuse
troops
revolution
battle
document
constitution
property

- Read the words on the list.
- Read the dialogue.
- Find the words.

> Who can tell me why people fought a **revolution** in the 1770s?

> People were against the British. They **refused** to obey the British king.

1. What Is Property?
Writing

The house in the picture is one kind of property. But property isn't just land. It can be clothing, books, furniture, tools for work, and other important items. What five items of property are most important for a family today? List your items. Explain why each is important. Show your partner what you have written.

2. Make a Chart
Graphic Organizer

Two events happened at the start of the Revolutionary War. Which do you think was more important? Ask five classmates. Tally their responses. Share your findings with your partner.

Event	Tally
Writing the Declaration of Independence	
Battles of Lexington and Concord	

3. Plan a Pamphlet
Writing

In the time of the Revolution, many people wrote pamphlets about important issues. What issue of today would you write a pamphlet about? Tell the topic of your pamphlet. Tell some of the points you would make. Show your idea to your partner.

4. What Are Your Rights?
Listening and Speaking

The Constitution is a document that lists your rights. With a partner, talk about the rights you have. Take turns describing them. Write them down. Share your list with your class.

New Americans, Then and Now

by Elsa MacGregor

People have always come to America looking for a better life. As early as the 1600s, people sailed to North America to find opportunities or freedoms that did not exist in their native lands. Many immigrants did well in the new country. Many also helped the country to do well.

One person who came to the American colonies as a young man was Alexander Hamilton. He was born in another British colony, the Caribbean island of Nevis. In 1772, the teenaged Hamilton came to New Jersey for his education. Hamilton became a strong supporter of the patriot cause. He fought in the Revolutionary War. After the war, he became a lawyer. He also helped found a bank. These were probably not opportunities he would have had on Nevis.

Hamilton was a key person in the planning of the U.S. **Constitution**. This document details the way our country's

government is set up. He was a member of the Constitutional Convention in 1787. He also wrote an important series of essays explaining why the Constitution should be ratified, or approved, by the states.

Hamilton is considered one of the Founding Fathers of the United States. He shows that immigrants to this country have often made lasting contributions.

Today, people come to the United States for many of the same reasons as they came in the past. Many come looking for jobs. These people believe that they will be able to live a better life here.

Other people come to escape oppressive governments in their native lands. They are looking for greater freedom.

People around the world have always thought of America as a land of opportunity. It's a place where they can work at better, higher paying jobs and where the quality of daily life is better than in many other countries.

Prove It

What are some ways Alexander Hamilton helped his new country?

My TWO Homes

As told by Clara Díaz
to Lynda Franco

In Guatemala, I lived with my mom and dad on a farm. One day, a letter arrived. I could see that my parents were very happy and excited. The letter said we would be able to move to the United States.

My uncle lived in the U.S., in the city of San Jose, California. He said *Mamá* and *Papá* could find good jobs there. We packed up our **property** and left.

Everything in the United States was new and exciting. My school had a lot of books in the classroom. We had computers, too. The walls were covered with pictures. I didn't speak much English yet, but I was learning fast! I wasn't the only new student in my class, either. Children from many other parts of the world were learning English along with me. Some of them, the ones from Mexico and El Salvador, spoke

Spanish, so we could help one another figure things out in this new city. We practiced our English together at lunchtime.

Most people in Guatemala live in the country. We live in a big city now. Everything is bigger and busier than back home on our farm. Some stores in San Jose are huge! I had never seen so many things to buy. There's a lot for families to do together, too. We love going to the city's museums and parks.

My mom got a job right away. She works in a hotel. My dad also found a job; he works building houses.

At first we lived with my uncle and my cousin. Then we found our own place to live nearby. We still get together for barbecues and baseball games in the park. I love my new life here in the United States!

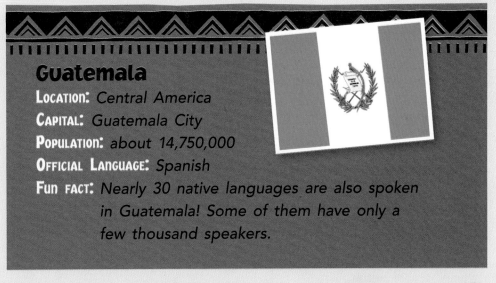

Guatemala

Location: Central America

Capital: Guatemala City

Population: about 14,750,000

Official Language: Spanish

Fun Fact: Nearly 30 native languages are also spoken in Guatemala! Some of them have only a few thousand speakers.

Retell "A Warning in Coal"

 One way to retell a story is to tell what the most important character does. This helps readers understand the story.

"A Warning in Coal" is a story about Jim, who is living in Boston during the time after the Boston Tea Party. Review the story on pages 36–41.

■ First Picture: What happens at the beginning of the story? What people do Jim meet on the street?

■ Second Picture: What task does Jim agree to help with? Why is it important?

■ Third Picture: How does Jim complete his task?

Use the pictures on page 49 to retell the story to your partner. As you tell about each part, point to the correct pictures. Use complete sentences.

Words you might use in your retelling:

British	Boston Tea Party	colony
troops	protest	liberty

Beginning

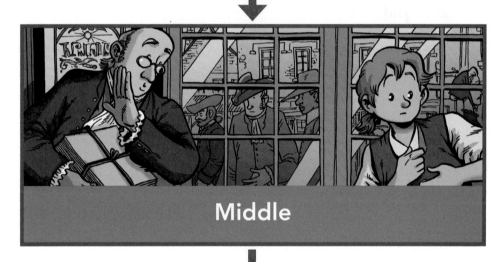

Middle

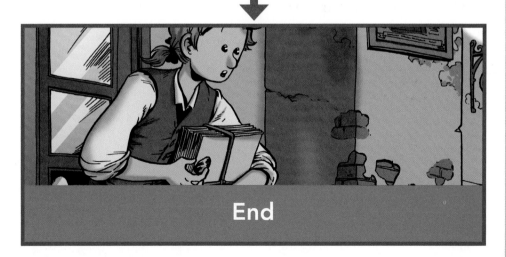

End

Dig Deeper

Look Back

Look at the two stories, "Early Thunder" and "A Warning in Coal." Answer these questions on a sheet of paper.

1. What do both stories have in common?
    Give one detail from each story that helps you know.

2. What is different about the two main characters, Daniel and Jim?

3. Which character from the other story would Daniel most likely get along with best? To *get along with* is to like or to agree with. Tell what details in the story helped you answer.

Talk About It

If you could create a monument, what would it look like?

Would it be a building? A statue? A garden?

Tell how you would create your monument.

Share with your classmates.

Do you all agree or disagree? Why or why not?

If people do not agree, how can you all work to come up with an agreement?

Conversation

> Sometimes you have to ask someone for help or permission. There is a polite way to ask for things. Use the word *please* when you ask. Say *thank you* when someone answers you or helps you.

Talk to a partner. One of you will be person A.
The other will be person B.

Person A   ## Person B

Ask to borrow something.

    Agree.

Ask for help in using the item.

    Tell how to use it.

Thank your partner.

    Reply.
    Say goodbye.

By the People

The **BIG** Question

How does our government help us?

☐ Why is the Constitution important?

☐ What are the parts of the United States government?

☐ How do the parts of the government work together?

1. What does good government do?

A good government…

☐ builds roads and bridges.

☐ makes sure there are enough schools.

☐ protects the country from outside attacks.

☐ makes fair laws.

2. In a democracy, how can people take part in their government?

People can take part in their government by…

☐ learning their rights and duties.

☐ writing a letter to lawmakers who represent them.

☐ voting.

☐ running for office.

3. Who are some of our government leaders?

National and local government leaders include…

☐ the President.

☐ senators.

☐ mayors.

☐ governors.

4. What does justice mean to you?

Justice means that…

☐ everyone has to obey the same laws.

☐ everyone has equal rights.

☐ if something goes wrong, people have a way to complain.

☐ if a law doesn't work well, there is a fair way to change it.

Say **more!**

Learn the Words

democracy
rights
political party
government
bill
Congress
veto
represent

Theme Vocabulary

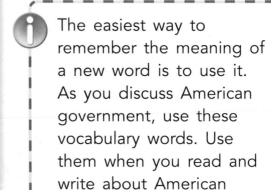

The easiest way to remember the meaning of a new word is to use it. As you discuss American government, use these vocabulary words. Use them when you read and write about American government, too.

Read the word.
Look at the picture.
Use the word in a sentence.

democracy

rights

political party

government

bill

Congress

veto

represent

Match the Pictures

Look at the pictures on the vocabulary cards. Choose two pictures that go together. Tell why you think the pictures go together.

On Trial

Graphic Novel

3 **Formal/Informal Language** "It cracked me up" means, "It made me laugh." Would you be more likely to use this expression when talking with friends or when talking to the principal?

Ladies and gentlemen of the jury, what is your verdict? Is Rosa guilty or not guilty?

13

Not guilty!

14

OK. Three red marks erased. Now I want to give you a new rule. It's as easy as pie to understand.

ROSA	xx
NESSA	xx
TODD	xxy
CHEN	x

15

Keep writing, but don't pass it on

16

13 Formal/Informal Language Mr. Valley is speaking as if he were in a courtroom. Does he use formal language or informal language?

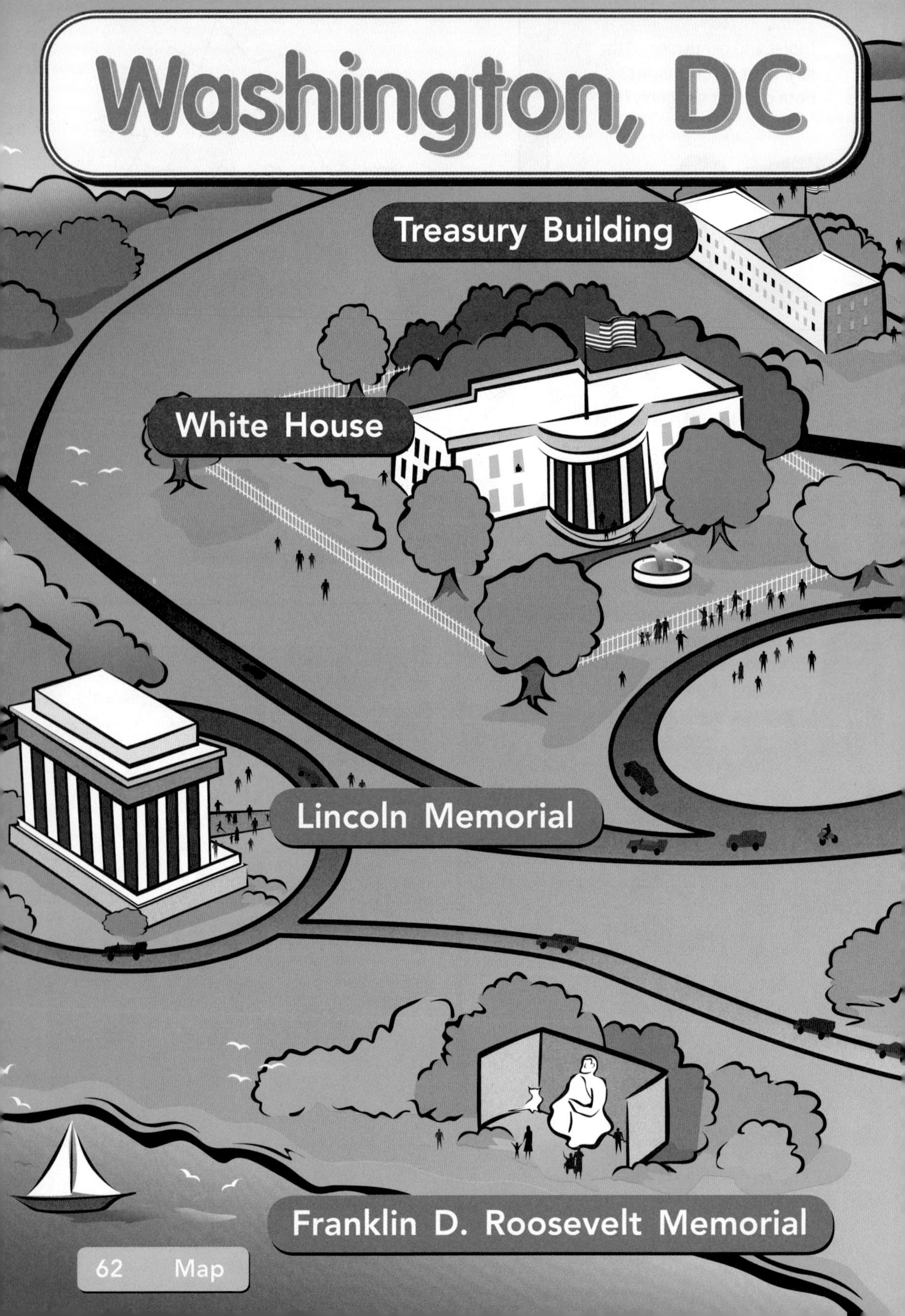

Washington, DC

Treasury Building

White House

Lincoln Memorial

Franklin D. Roosevelt Memorial

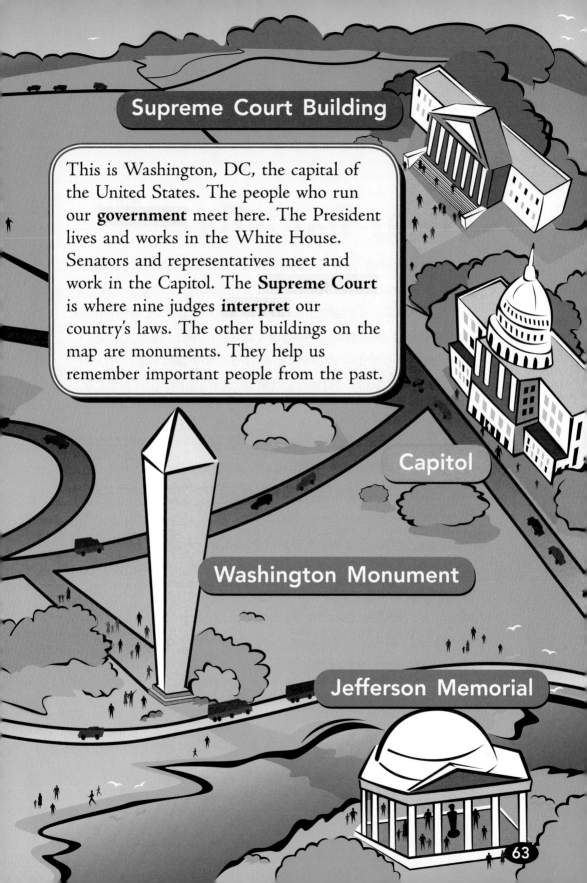

Supreme Court Building

This is Washington, DC, the capital of the United States. The people who run our **government** meet here. The President lives and works in the White House. Senators and representatives meet and work in the Capitol. The **Supreme Court** is where nine judges **interpret** our country's laws. The other buildings on the map are monuments. They help us remember important people from the past.

Capitol

Washington Monument

Jefferson Memorial

Friendly Letter

Dear Daniella,

April 5

I'm sending you a copy of an article about wolves from *Nature News for Kids*. Just look at the photo of the two wolves standing in the snow. Don't they look exactly like our dogs—yours and mine? As soon as I saw it I thought—Wow, how did they get a photo of Henry and Molly? Then I started reading the article, which upset me a lot.

It looks like our state is going to pass a law that takes the gray wolf off the endangered list. Can you believe it? That's the same as putting it on the extinction list!

It's not like I would welcome the chance to meet a wolf face to face, but that's not the point. Remember what Ms. Demerest told us in Science? She said that when a species becomes extinct, the ecosystem is knocked off balance because everything in nature is connected to everything else.

So, who wants to get rid of wolves? Mostly, it's the ranchers and the hunters. The ranchers say the wolves are killing off their livestock. The hunters say the wolves are killing off the wild elks. Both groups want the wolf population to go away. This would be really bad for the wolves, of course. But it would hurt the ecosystem, too.

I don't know if we can do anything to stop this law, but maybe we can organize a letter campaign. Maybe if we send enough letters to our state senators and representatives, we can help change the laws. Read the article and tell me what do you think. Then we'll talk. I am keeping my fingers crossed.

Anyway, I miss you a lot! And hope to see you and Molly soon!

Until next time,

María Elena

65

Presidents of the United States

The President is the head of the government. Our country has had more than 40 Presidents since it was founded. They come from different **political parties**.

Adams, John

John Adams was our second President, serving from 1797 to 1801. He was the first President to live in the White House. Even before the Revolutionary War, he was a leader in our country's fight for independence from Britain. He also advised the authors of the Constitution, the document that established **democracy** in the United States.

Bush, George W.

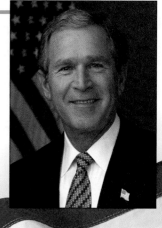

George W. Bush was our forty-third President. He served for two terms, from 2001 to 2009. Before he was President, he was the governor of Texas. His dad was also named George Bush. He was once President, too! George W. Bush worked on policies to improve the nation's educational standards.

Jefferson, Thomas

Thomas Jefferson was our third President, serving from 1801 to 1809. He was the main author of the Declaration of Independence. Jefferson was the President who added the Louisiana Territory to the United States. This large area of land was bought from France. Jefferson spoke many languages besides English.

Kennedy, John F.

John F. Kennedy was our thirty-fifth President, serving from 1961 to 1963. While Kennedy was President, African Americans were protesting for their civil **rights**. Kennedy worked with civil rights leaders to get new laws passed. He also began the Peace Corps, an organization that sent young volunteers to other countries to increase understanding between cultures.

Lincoln, Abraham

Abraham Lincoln was our sixteenth President. He served from 1861 to 1865. He was President during the American Civil War. That war lasted for four years— almost Lincoln's entire presidency. Because of how he kept the country strong during those years, Lincoln is considered one of our greatest Presidents.

Madison, James

James Madison was our fourth President, from 1809 to 1817. He helped write the Bill of Rights, an addition to the Constitution that guarantees citizens important rights. The Bill of Rights says that all Americans have the right to freedom of speech, freedom of religion, and the right to a fair trial. He was a congressman in the House of Representatives. He **represented** the state of Virginia.

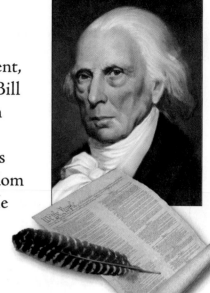

Obama, Barack

Barack Obama became our forty-fourth President in 2009. He was the first African American to be elected President. He appointed two women to the Supreme Court. One of them, Sonia Sotomayor, was the first Latina ever to serve on the Supreme Court.

Reagan, Ronald

Ronald Reagan was our fortieth President, from 1981 to 1989. He was once a movie actor, but then he got interested in politics. He was the governor of California before he became President. Reagan signed a treaty with the Soviet Union that banned some very dangerous weapons. He appointed the first woman to the Supreme Court, Sandra Day O'Connor.

Roosevelt, Franklin D.

Franklin D. Roosevelt was our thirty-second President, from 1933 to 1945. Roosevelt was President during the Great Depression. He worked hard so that many people could get jobs. He was also President during World War II. He helped the United States win that war. His wife, Eleanor, was very active in politics as well. She worked for the rights of all people.

Roosevelt, Theodore

Theodore Roosevelt was our twenty-sixth President, from 1901 to 1909. He was a cousin of Franklin D. Roosevelt. He was concerned about the environment and created many national parks. Theodore Roosevelt signed the Pure Food and Drug Act into law. This was the first American law that controlled what could be put into foods that were sold.

Washington, George

George Washington was our country's very first President, serving from 1789 to 1797. That is why he is often called "the father of our country." Before he became President, he helped lead the fight for independence from Britain in the Revolutionary War.

Freedom

★ ★

by Lynelle H. Morgenthaler

Freedom.
Can you smell it?
Can you taste it?
Can you see it?

Freedom is the air we breathe.
It is the food we eat.
It is the company we keep.

It is the words in our mouths.
It is the prayer we make.
It is the privacy we stake.

Our Bill of Rights lets us know
Just how far we can go.
Ten rights that keep us free—
You and me!

Justice

★ ★ ★ ★ ★ ★ ★ ★ ★ ★ ★ ★ ★ ★ ★ ★

by Andrew Miller

When all of us
follow the same laws
Then there is **justice**

When all of us
have the same rights
Then there is justice

When all of us
are judged the same
Then there is justice

When all of us
can say what we believe
When all of us
can work and can achieve
Then there is justice

Sometimes we must fight
for what is fair
when others do not
seem to care
And when we do
Then there is justice

WHY DO WE HAVE A Constitution?

by Judy Rosenbaum

Our country was started by people who gained independence from Britain and its king, George III. A king is not elected. He usually becomes king because his father was king before him. He rules for his whole life.

Besides King George, Britain had a governing body called a parliament. The most powerful members of parliament were dukes and lords. Their fathers had been dukes and lords. Their sons would be dukes and lords after them.

Americans didn't want their government to work that way. They didn't want power to be in the hands of just a few people. They didn't want their country to be run by a lifelong ruler. They certainly didn't want power to be passed down from father to son to grandson. Americans wanted a democracy. This means that the citizens can vote people into and out of the government.

At first, Americans didn't even want one single government. They chose to be mostly independent states. The states were joined together by a weak central government. A document called the Articles of Confederation set up that system.

By 1786, the system was in huge trouble. States couldn't agree on anything. Many states didn't even send money to fund the central government. As a result, the country couldn't afford an army or navy to protect itself.

By this time, nearly everyone realized that something had to change. Some people believed that without a strong government, the United States would fall apart. Other countries would seize pieces of it, and Americans would be ruled by kings again.

In May 1787, representatives from the states met in Philadelphia, Pennsylvania. They argued about what kind of government to set up. The product of their arguments was a document called the Constitution. The Constitution is the highest law of the United States. No laws can be made that go against the Constitution.

This early American flag shows that the country had fewer states in 1787.

Here are some of the things the Constitution sets forth.

- It names the positions, or offices, of the government, such as the President.
- It describes the powers that each office holder has. Power is spread among different office holders and different parts of government.
- It tells how each office holder is chosen and how long a term each office holder is allowed to serve.
- It tells how the government makes and enforces laws.
- It even tells how the Constitution itself can be changed. Amendments can be added to give new rights, powers, or limits to the government or the people.

Many people still did not want a stronger government. So the writers of the Constitution added one more part to the document. They wrote the first ten amendments. Each one protected certain rights of the American people. For instance, the First Amendment protects people's right to choose their

The Constitution was signed by many of the people who helped write it.

religion. These ten amendments are called the Bill of Rights.

Once the Bill of Rights was added, the Constitution was approved by the states. It became the law of the United States in 1789.

After the Constitution set up the rules for a national government, the government could then start doing its jobs. It could protect the rights and the safety of Americans. It could make laws that applied to the whole country, not just to one state.

Since 1789, other amendments have been added to the Constitution. Amendments like these have allowed the country to keep growing and adapting to the needs of the people.

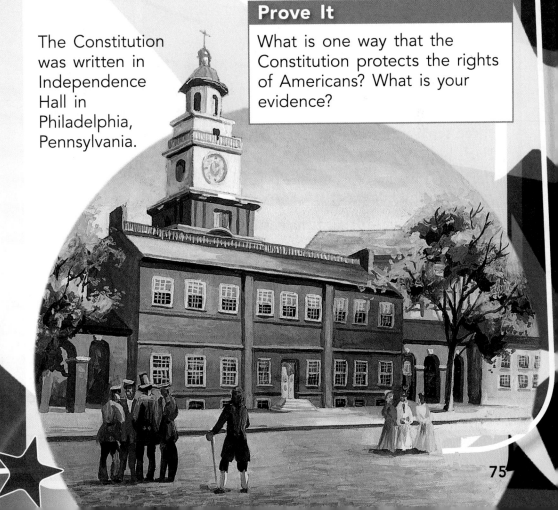

The Constitution was written in Independence Hall in Philadelphia, Pennsylvania.

Prove It

What is one way that the Constitution protects the rights of Americans? What is your evidence?

How Our Government Works

by Omar Wilkins

Our democracy is a representative democracy. This means that the people in the government represent the people who elected them.

The Constitution tells how our government is set up. The planners of the Constitution did not want to place too much power in any one part of the government. That is why they organized our government into three separate branches. Each branch has a different function. Each branch also makes sure the other two branches follow the law. This system of **checks and balances** ensures that no one branch becomes too powerful. In order for the government to work, people in the different branches must **cooperate** with one another.

The
LEGISLATIVE BRANCH
makes new laws.

The
EXECUTIVE BRANCH
enforces laws.

The
JUDICIAL BRANCH
interprets the meaning of the laws.

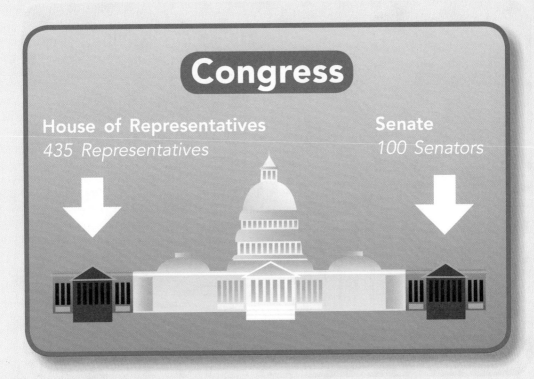

Congress

House of Representatives
435 Representatives

Senate
100 Senators

The **legislative branch** is our **Congress**. Congress has two parts: the House of Representatives and the Senate.

A state's number of representatives depends on its population. States such as California have large populations. These states have a lot of representatives in the House. Other states have fewer representatives. Some states have just one representative.

In the Senate, each state, large or small, has two senators. That makes 100 senators in all.

Before a law is passed, it is known as a **bill**. Senators and representatives write the bill. They also vote on it to make it into a law. The members of Congress talk to one another and debate every bill. Since they belong to different political parties and have different ideas, it's sometimes hard for them to cooperate to make laws.

The Capitol Building

After a bill passes in Congress, it is sent to the President. The President is the head of the **executive branch**. The President must sign the bill to make it into a law. If the President does not like the bill, he or she can **veto** it. Then it goes back to Congress to be changed.

Sometimes the senators and representatives make the changes that the President wants.

Sometimes the senators and representatives do not agree with the President. If they work together, they can vote to override the President's veto. That means that the bill becomes a law even though the President did not sign it. These actions all show how checks and balances work.

The White House

The President has other jobs, too. Here are some of them:

+ Defending our country. The President is in charge of the armed forces.

+ Deciding how the United States gets along with other countries. The President can appoint ambassadors (people who represent the wishes and business interests of the United States in other countries).

+ Overseeing how the government is run. The President has to help plan the nation's budget. This collection of document tells how money will be spent all through the government.

+ Acting in emergencies. The President can decide to send troops or government aid following a flood or other events.

Zoom In

Why are checks and balances important to our government? What evidence tells you?

The Supreme Court is part of the **judicial branch** of government. There are many courts in the country, but the Supreme Court is the highest court of all. The nine Supreme Court justices listen to cases and interpret laws. The justices do this by deciding if a law goes against the Constitution. If it does, the Supreme Court can strike down the law. This action shows how the Supreme Court limits the powers of the other two branches of government.

The President, the members of Congress, and the Supreme Court justices have often disagreed on exactly how to make, carry out, or interpret the law. In a democracy, people will not always agree about the best way to run a country. Sometimes,

The Supreme Court Building

members of the government have even reversed decisions made earlier in our history. For example, in 1896, the Supreme Court said that it was legal to prevent people of different races from going to the same public schools. In 1954, a different group of Supreme Court justices ruled that this was not legal. From then on, all Americans have been able to attend the same schools.

All these members of government have one thing in common. When they take office, the President, the senators, the representatives, and the justices each take an oath of office. In different wording, each of them swears to uphold and defend the Constitution of the United States.

Prove It

What details show how the Constitution is important to our government?

Fighting Words

A mystery by Janet Orosco

CHAPTER 1

Simon Chang was falling asleep. History lessons did that to him, even though he liked his teacher, Mrs. Armstrong. Although he liked school, he couldn't understand why he had to study the *past*. What did cowboys and miners and railroads have to do with him? The important things were happening *now*, right here, in Washington, DC, his hometown. He sat up straight and tried to pay attention. Then the final bell rang and he was free.

Simon lived close enough to walk home every afternoon. He was glad he didn't have to catch the city bus that stopped half a block away. Sometimes he would notice the riders waiting in line, and they often looked tired or impatient. Today, though, he noticed a man at the back of the line who looked quite peaceful and calm. The man stood very straight, and he had shiny black hair. From the back, he seemed about the age of Simon's father, but Simon noticed that he moved slowly. Maybe he was older than he looked.

Just as the man was opening his wallet to pay the fare, a woman rushed up. At the door, she accidentally bumped into the man and knocked his wallet out of his hands. Money, a credit card, and slips of paper spilled out in all directions. Simon joined a handful of people to help gather up the scattered belongings and return them to the man.

But after the bus pulled away, Simon saw something else lying on the ground. He bent to pick it up. It was a square photograph, black and white with small scalloped edges. He looked up, but he was too late. The bus was out of sight. Simon carefully tucked the photo between the pages of his math book and hurried home.

When Simon got home, his dad, who taught Chinese at a nearby college, was already there. Simon eagerly showed him the photo and asked for advice about finding the man. Dad's first suggestion was to call the police. "Maybe there's something in the photo that would allow the police to identify the man," Dad said.

But when Simon called, the police officer asked if a crime had taken place. When Simon said no, the officer said he was sorry but the police were too busy to act as a lost-and-found agency.

Simon tried not to be discouraged. He stared harder at the photo, looking for clues. "The man in the picture is holding up a notebook, but I can't make out what it says."

His father took a magnifying glass from his desk. "Try this."

"Wow!" Simon's face lit up. "This is great. Every letter is clear!" But a minute later he looked worried again. The notebook page in the photo was filled with strange words. They weren't in any language he had ever seen. "Dad," he said. "Maybe these words are some kind of code. I think the man in the photo might be a spy!"

"Just holding a codebook doesn't make you a spy," said Dad. "Don't jump to conclusions. Let's see if we can find some facts instead." He suggested taking the photo to class the next day and seeing if Simon's teacher had any ideas about the photo.

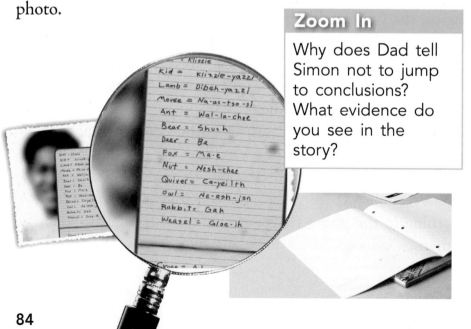

Zoom In

Why does Dad tell Simon not to jump to conclusions? What evidence do you see in the story?

CHAPTER 2

Simon had never been so eager to see Mrs. Armstrong! He made sure to arrive at school before the class started. The first thing Mrs. Armstrong did was something neither Simon nor his father had thought of. She turned the picture over! On the back, the year *1968* was written.

1968

"This gives me an idea," she said. "Tomorrow, you and your father should go to the National Museum of the American Indian. Ask to see the person in charge of the archives. That's a collection of historical documents. Ask if someone can help you identify the man in this photograph. And on Monday, Detective Chang, you will report your findings to the class!"

Simon and his dad were the first ones in line when the museum opened the next day. They went straight to the archives. The man who met them studied the photo with his own magnifying glass. He recognized the picture at once. In 2001, the man in the photo had received the Congressional Medal, along with other Navajo Indians, for service in World War II as code talkers.

The archivist explained that the code talkers were Native Americans who helped the U.S. by developing codes that no one else could figure out. Various Native American peoples, including the Navajo, Comanche, and Cherokee, each developed a code based on their own language. They memorized these codes and used them to send radio transmissions. The Navajo language was especially useful for this task because it had no written form at that time. Other Indian languages had very few words in writing. The languages were passed down orally from one generation to the next. Almost no outsiders had any way to learn the languages.

Simon was speechless, and the archivist chuckled at the boy's surprise. "Did you have any idea that you were holding a

photo of an American war hero? These events took place around seventy years ago. But the code was so secret it was classified by the military. The code talkers were not allowed to tell *anyone* what they had done until the operation was declassified in 1968. That's why the date on this photo was helpful. That's when, the code talkers could finally reveal their secret to the public."

The archivist went into his office and came back smiling. "I've set up a meeting. This gentleman would be honored if you and your dad would visit him at his home tomorrow so he could thank you in person for returning the photograph. He's ninety-one years old now, and that's the only picture of him and his codebook that his family has. His family is so grateful to you for taking the trouble to track him down."

On Monday, Simon Chang presented his report to the class. His classmates started calling him "The Detective." After that, he never felt so bored with history.

Prove It

Does Simon think that Mrs. Armstrong is more helpful in Chapter 1 or Chapter 2? What evidence helped you answer?

Learn the Words

executive branch
judicial branch
legislative branch
checks and balances
cooperate
Supreme Court
interpret
justice

- Read the words on the list.
- Read the dialogue.
- Find the words.

Sorry to be late!

The two U.S. congressmen are speaking about the **legislative branch** of the government.

Thank you for answering my question, Congressman.

1. You Are the Reporter
Writing

Suppose you are a reporter. You will interview one of the speakers in the picture. Think of five questions about that person's job in the U.S. Congress. Share your questions with your partner. Talk about how your questions could be improved.

2. Make a Chart
Graphic Organizer

Ask some classmates which branch of the government they would like to work in. Tally their responses. Share your findings with your partner.

Which branch of the government would you like to work in?	
executive branch	
legislative branch	
judicial branch	

3. Make a Drawing
Listening and Speaking

How can people or groups cooperate to get something done? Think of something in your community that you think needs to be improved. What task needs to be done? Make a drawing. Show people working together on that task. Tell your partner about your drawing.

4. Speak Out
Listening and Speaking

Good laws will establish justice in a community of any size. What would be a just law for a school to have? Prepare a speech. You could tell about a law that a school could make. You might tell about a law that your school already has. Make your speech to the class.

Oscar Gutierrez

by Marilee Robin Burton

This is Oscar Gutierrez. He immigrated to the United States from Mexico. He came to the United State to find a good job and to have a better life.

Oscar knows how cars work. He got a job repairing cars and trucks. At first he didn't have much money. But he worked very hard. He tried not to spend too much money. Instead, he saved and saved.

After a few years, he had enough money to start his own business. Today he is his own boss. Now he helps new immigrants. He hires them to work in his own shop. He even has enough money to send some to his parents and grandparents in Mexico. Many immigrants from different countries send money home to their families to help out.

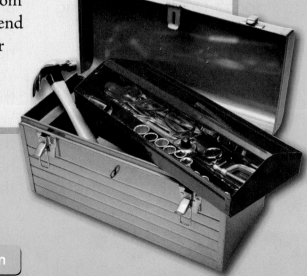

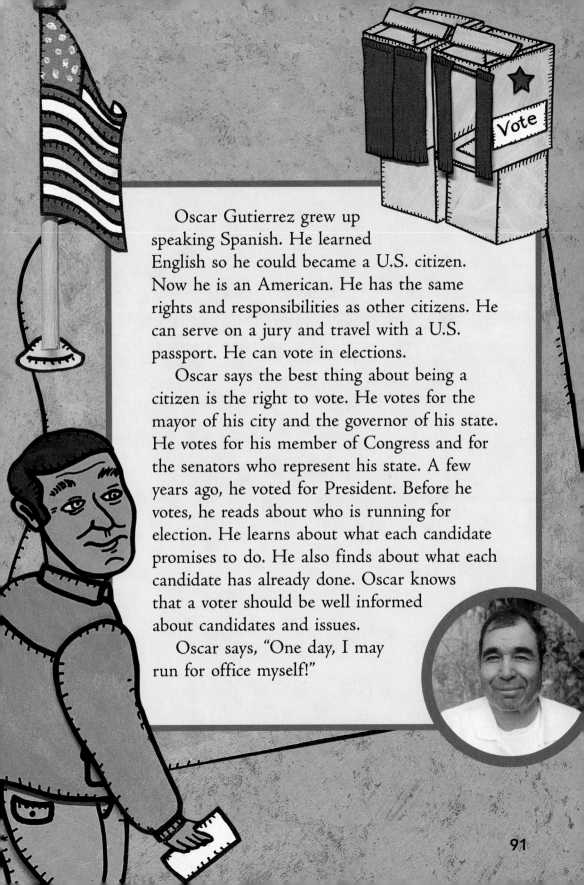

Oscar Gutierrez grew up speaking Spanish. He learned English so he could became a U.S. citizen. Now he is an American. He has the same rights and responsibilities as other citizens. He can serve on a jury and travel with a U.S. passport. He can vote in elections.

Oscar says the best thing about being a citizen is the right to vote. He votes for the mayor of his city and the governor of his state. He votes for his member of Congress and for the senators who represent his state. A few years ago, he voted for President. Before he votes, he reads about who is running for election. He learns about what each candidate promises to do. He also finds about what each candidate has already done. Oscar knows that a voter should be well informed about candidates and issues.

Oscar says, "One day, I may run for office myself!"

How Does a Bill Become a Law?

• • •

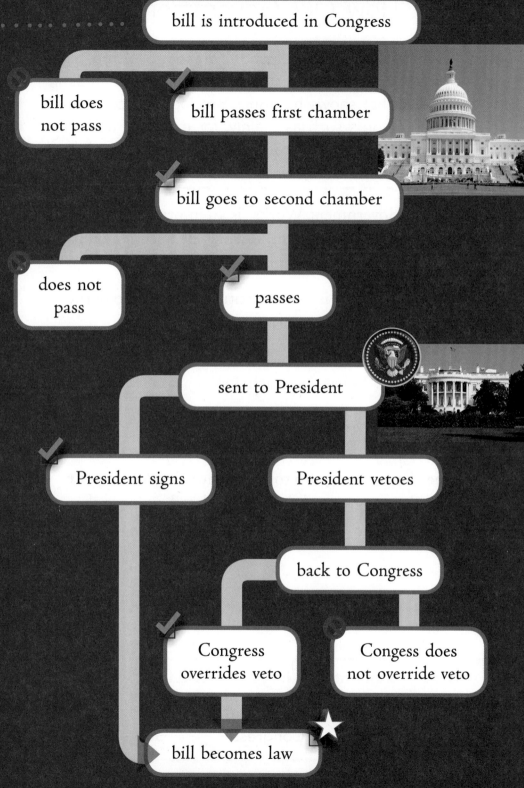

bill is introduced in Congress

bill does not pass

bill passes first chamber

bill goes to second chamber

does not pass

passes

sent to President

President signs

President vetoes

back to Congress

Congress overrides veto

Congess does not override veto

bill becomes law

Retell "How Our Government Works"

> When you retell a selection, present only the important ideas and details. Present these ideas in a way that shows how they are logically connected. Using words such as *mainly, for example,* and *including* will help readers understand what the selection is mostly about.

"How Our Government Works" is an informational article. It tells about our government. Review the selection on pages 76–81. Look at the chart on page 95.

■ **Top Picture:** Why is the Constitution at the top of the chart? Tell what its importance is.

■ **Middle Row of Pictures:** What are the three branches of government? What does each do?

■ **Bottom Row of Pictures:** What is an example from each branch? What powers does each one have?

Use the chart on page 95 to retell the selection to your partner. As you give each important detail, point to the correct picture. Use complete sentences.

Words you might use in your retelling:

executive branch	judicial branch	legislative branch
bill	Congress	Supreme Court

Constitution

Legislative Branch

Executive Branch

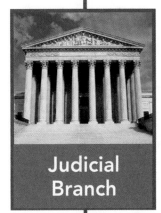

Judicial Branch

Congress

President

Justices

Dig Deeper

Look Back

Work with a partner. Look back at "Why Do We Have a Constitution?" and "How Our Government Works." In both selections, find information about the executive branch, the legislative branch, and the judicial branch. Use this information to answer the following questions:

1. What member of the government is the head of the executive branch?

2. Who decides if a law goes against the Constitution?

3. What part of the government is divided into two parts?

4. Who, besides the President, is elected?

Each partner should write his or her answers on a sheet of paper.

Talk About It

Oscar Gutierrez immigrated to the United States.

First, he got a job repairing cars.

At the beginning, he didn't have much money.

Then, he saved and saved his money.

Finally, he was able to start his own business.

Tell about another person or event. Use words such as *first, then,* and *finally.*

Conversation

Use the words *have to*, *must*, or *should* to tell about things that someone needs to do. When you order someone to do something, be polite. You might thank the person who carries out the order.

Talk to a partner. One of you will be person A. The other will be person B.

Person A   **Person B**

Tell your partner to
do a task.

Agree. Ask what else
must be done.

Thank your partner.
Give another order.

Ask for help.

Agree to help.

Thank your partner.

Now Hear This!

The **BIG** Question

How does sound affect your life every day?

☐ What are some ways in which musical instruments around the world are alike?

☐ How can music change the way people feel?

☐ How do animals use sounds to help them survive?

1. What things make sounds?

Sounds can be made by…

- ☐ machines.
- ☐ objects bumping together.
- ☐ musical instruments.
- ☐ the wind.
- ☐ falling objects.
- ☐ living things.

2. What are some ways to describe sounds?

Sounds can be…

- ☐ loud or soft.
- ☐ clear or muffled.
- ☐ high-pitched or low-pitched.
- ☐ rattling.
- ☐ whispery.
- ☐ echoing.

3. What kinds of musical instruments do you like?

I like musical instruments that…

☐ are loud.

☐ have a high-pitched sound.

☐ make noise when I strike them.

☐ have strings.

4. How can people make music on different instruments?

People can…

☐ blow on a wind instrument.

☐ shake or strike a percussion instrument.

☐ blow on a brass instrument.

☐ pluck a string instrument with their fingers.

Say **more!**

Learn the Words

vibration
eardrum
sound waves
beat
note
volume
amplify
muffle

Theme Vocabulary

The easiest way to remember the meaning of a new word is to use it. As you discuss sound and music, use these vocabulary words. Use them when you read and write about sound and music, too.

Read the word.
Look at the picture.
Use the word in a sentence.

vibration

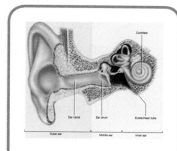

eardrum

sound waves

beat

note

volume

amplify

muffle

How Do You Feel?

Look at the vocabulary cards. Choose one picture and tell how it makes you feel.

A Special Bird

Ramon, see that black bird? It's as thin as a rail.

He's not digging up enough worms and bugs to eat.

1

Maybe he can't. I think the dirt in our yard is too hard.

Let's give that bird a break and dig up some food for it.

2

Look, Maya, I'm an early bird. I caught a worm.

Ha Ha! Leave it out for him.

3

Let's call him Bert.

Bert got it!

4

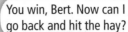

6:00 A.M. the next morning...

RAP RAP RAP RAP

Bert! Go away. I need my shuteye.

monday

5

You win, Bert. Now can I go back and hit the hay?

6

RAP RAP RAP

tuesday

Stop it Bert. I need my beauty sleep.

6:00

7

8

5 Formal/Informal Language How could Ramon say "I need my shuteye" in a more formal way?

Expressions Maya and Ramon try to blow Bert away with the fan. "To blow off" someone is also an expression that means "to ignore or drive away" the person.

106

14) **Formal/Informal Language** "You can't win 'em all" is another way to say "You can't win all the time." Is this expression formal or informal language?

The Drum

by Nikki Giovanni

daddy says the world is
a drum tight and hard
and i told him
i'm gonna **beat**
out my own rhythm

LISTEN TO THE BEAT

by Susan Meyers

Listen to me now.
Here's what I have to say.
Music is sound.
You can make it any way.
Clap your hands.
Beat a drum.
Vibrations in the air
Make your **eardrums** hum.
Turn the **volume** up.
Your whole head aches.

Turn it down!
Give your ears a break!
Listen for the **pitch**—
Is it high? Is it low?
Get it just right,
And the music flows.
Feel the catchy beat.
Tap it with your feet.
Boom ta-da! Boom ta-da!
Listen to the sounds!

The  Lesson

by Sabrina Nelson

One day when I was three, I hopped onto the piano bench and played "Happy Birthday." At age seven, I started performing. Music was my whole life.

One day when I was eight, my piano teacher, Madame Schlossnagel, told me to audition for the Young Musicians Competition in Washington, DC. The winner would get a big scholarship and a chance to play in our town's orchestra.

From then on, I practiced my piece two or three hours every day. I hummed it in my sleep. I drummed it on my desk. My life had shrunk down to the size of a keyboard.

The audition went well. There was nothing to do but go home and plan my letter of acceptance.

Well, I didn't win. I was crushed. Music had let me down. It was like having your best friend tell you she had never actually liked you in the first place. I quit piano and joined the swim team.

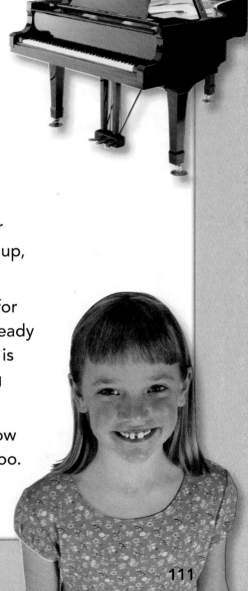

One day I got home to find my old music teacher in the kitchen. She was talking to my mom. My teacher asked if I could give lessons to a little boy. Thomas didn't like to talk, but he loved music. I said I'd like that.

I don't know if it was my mom or Madame Schlossnagel who set this up, but it was great that it happened.

I've been working with Thomas for about a year now. We are getting ready for a four-handed piano sonata. He is making great progress. He's talking better, too.

I still want to be a pianist, but now there's so much else I want to do, too. The important thing is that music is back in my life.

A WORLD OF MUSIC

by Manuel Vargas

Every culture in the world has musical instruments. Some instruments have been around for thousands of years. Some are much newer.

You can classify most instruments by how you produce the sound on them. Do you pluck part of it? Do you blow into it? Do you hit it? Here are some **string instruments**, **wind instruments**, **brass instruments**, and **percussion instruments** from around the world.

String Instruments

A string instrument has one or more strings stretched across it. When the strings are plucked, hit, or rubbed with a bow, they vibrate, or move very quickly. The vibrations create sounds. On most string instruments, each string is tuned to a different **note**. So you might hear notes with a high pitch or with a low pitch.

balalaika

charango

sitar

Some string instruments that are plucked are the balalaika from Russia, the charango from South America, the sitar from India, and the pipa from East Asia. A string instrument that is played with a bow is the violin. This instrument began in Europe but is played in many countries today.

didgeridoo

Many kinds of string instruments are made out of wood. Some are made from animal shells or gourds. The strings can be made out of many kinds of materials, including plant fibers, metal wire, plastic, and nylon.

Wind Instruments

chirimía

Wind instruments are a hollow tube with holes carved out. A player blows into the tube or into a mouthpiece attached to the tube. Many wind instruments have one or two small reeds on or inside the mouthpiece. The vibration of the reeds helps produce the sound. To change the pitch, a player covers and uncovers the holes on the side.

quena

Around the world, you'll find wind instruments made of all kinds of materials. The didgeridoo of Australia is usually made from a hollowed-out tree branch. The quena from South America is made of bamboo.

Brass Instruments

trumpet

Brass instruments such as trumpets, tubas, and other horns are really a kind of wind instrument. (Wind instruments that are not made of metal are usually called woodwinds.) You can guess from their name that brasses are made of metal. Like all wind instruments, they are hollow tubes of air that players blow into.

Percussion Instruments

Percussion instruments include drums of all sizes and shapes, cymbals, rattles, and xylophones. There are many ways to make a sound on percussion instruments. Players tap or beat some instruments with their hands. Other instruments are struck with a beater, such as a drumstick. Still other instruments are made of pieces that are struck against each other. Imagine all the different sounds these instruments can make!

gong

There is probably a greater variety of shape among percussion instruments than among other kinds of instruments. String instruments need to have strings stretched somewhere across them. Wind and brass instruments have a hollow tube. Percussion instruments just need something that can be hit or shaken. A percussion instrument can be a big round brass gong; a tall, cylinder-shaped drum; two sticks hit together; or even a rattle made from a hollow gourd.

Percussion instruments can be some of the loudest instruments of all. Big drums such as kettledrums or Japanese taiko drums make a booming sound. The metal gongs of Asia can produce a super-high volume of sound.

Today there are a lot of other loud musical instruments. That's because of electric speakers and microphones. So you really have to be careful to protect your eardrums. Listening to very loud music can damage your hearing. And you want to keep your hearing sharp throughout your life!

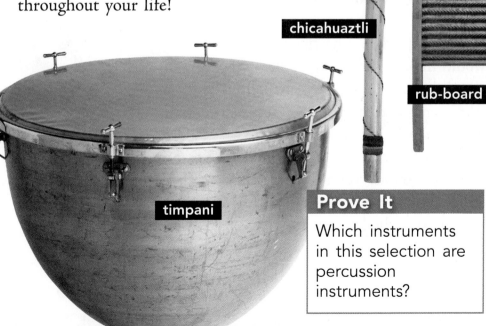

güiro

chicahuaztli

rub-board

timpani

Prove It

Which instruments in this selection are percussion instruments?

115

String Instruments Through the Years

by Molly Wheeler

A lot of today's musical instruments are relatives of the instruments of long ago. String instruments are a good example.

HARPS

Harps were played in ancient India, Egypt, and China. It is thought that the idea for a harp came from a bow and arrow. This makes a lot of sense. To shoot an arrow, a hunter had to pull back the bowstring and release it quickly. The tight string would make a twanging sound. So people made a hard, bow-shaped frame and stretched strings across it. They soon found that strings of different lengths would each make a different sound. Today's harps are still a frame with strings of different lengths stretched across them.

VIOLINS AND GUITARS

Violins and guitars both have a long neck. Strings are stretched tightly across the body and the neck. The hollow, air-filled body acts like an echo chamber. The trapped air enriches the sounds made by the strings. We say it makes the sound more resonant.

A kind of violin was played in Europe and western Asia by about A.D. 900. Violins reached their present-day form by about 1700.

The earliest form of guitar might have developed in ancient Greece. Through the centuries, changes such as steel strings improved the sound.

The next big change for guitars arrived by the early 1930s—electricity! The electric guitar could produce a more powerful sound than any guitar before it. Electric guitars don't have a hollow body. They don't need air to **amplify** their sound!

Nowadays the sound of any instrument can be created digitally on a computer. Now anyone can play an entire orchestra!

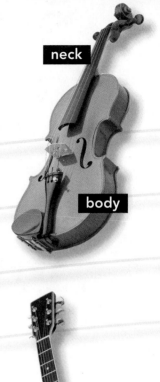

neck

body

neck

body

Prove It

What evidence shows that string instruments began very long ago?

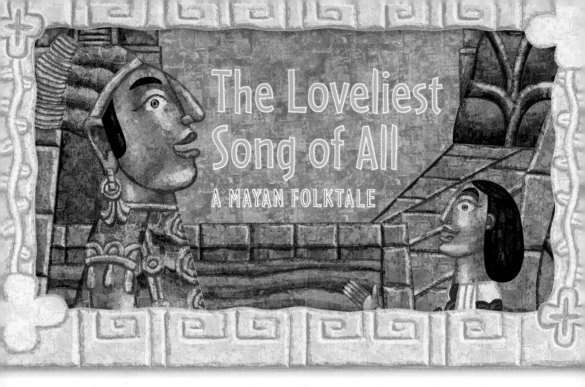

The Loveliest Song of All
A MAYAN FOLKTALE

retold by Sonia W. Black

Thousands of years ago in the land of the Maya, a king and his young daughter lived in a magnificent palace. The king adored his beautiful daughter, and she loved her father dearly. The two of them spent many happy times together.

As the years passed and the princess grew older, however, a great change came over her. The princess, who had always been so cheerful, grew very sad. The king was truly puzzled. He tried everything he could think of to lift her spirits and make her happy once more.

The king ordered fancy gifts for her. He had the people of his court find jewelry made of jade, shells, and gold. He had them weave dresses of the most beautiful colors. He even gathered children to play games to entertain her.

Nothing helped.

> **Zoom In**
>
> Who are the main characters so far? Describe them.

The princess remained glum. She would not laugh. She would not sing. She would not play. She barely talked. Many days she refused to leave her chamber.

Her father was overcome with worry. "I've tried *everything*," he cried. "What else must I do?"

Finally, the king sought the counsel of his advisors. When the advisors appeared before him, the king said, "I've tried everything to make my daughter happy, but she continues to be sad," he explained. "Please tell me, what must I do?"

The advisors consulted with each other. Then they approached the king with their answer.

"The princess has become a young woman," the advisors explained. "When she finds her life's companion, she will be joyous again."

"A-ha!" exclaimed the king. "I will order the people of my court to begin a search for a suitable husband at once!"

The king's command was carried out at once. People sped from the palace and traveled throughout the land. They looked far and wide for the perfect match for the princess.

The travelers returned to the palace. Proudly, they presented the king with a list containing the names of all the noble young men in the kingdom.

The king declared, "You will be richly rewarded if the princess finds favor with one of these candidates and he erases her sadness."

The king didn't waste any time. He invited every one of the noble young men to visit the palace. The men arrived wearing colorful robes and ornaments. Each young noble looked handsome or seemed strong and talented. Filled with hope, the king presented the men to his daughter.

Not one of them could get the princess's attention!

Suddenly everyone heard the faint sound of singing. A young man was approaching. As he got closer, everyone could see that he was simply dressed.

"Certainly he is not one of the invited noble young men!" said the king.

As the young man came closer, his singing became louder. Its beauty so astounded people that they grew quiet and still. Slowly their attention turned to the princess. They were shocked. The princess was no longer looking gloomy and sad. She had begun to do a joyful dance!

"Your song is beautiful," said the princess, "but it does not compare to the birds' songs. If you can learn to sing like the birds, I will marry you."

The young man declared, "Dear Princess, in three full moons, I will do it!"

Zoom In

How does the princess change when she hears the young man's music? What details helped you know?

The young man departed to the forest. "All of nature's birds are here among the trees," he said. "What better place is there for me to learn to sing as they do?"

For two months in the forest, the young man tried to sing like the birds, but he couldn't.

One night, he cried out in frustration. "This is impossible! I want to win the princess's heart with my song. But how can that ever happen when I still can't sing like the birds?"

Suddenly, the Spirit of the Woods appeared. "I will help you win your bride," the spirit promised.

The young man was startled. He gladly accepted the help offered by the spirit.

The spirit hollowed out a tree branch and poked holes in its side. Then he told the young man that he should blow through one end. By covering and uncovering the holes, the young man could make different musical sounds from the vibrating air.

For the next month, the young man experimented with his new instrument. He called it a *chirimía*. He learned to play high notes and low notes on his *chirimía*. The sound was extraordinary. Even the birds listened to him, and they chirped their praise.

The young man played with joy because he knew that now, thanks to his *chirimía*, he really did sound like the birds.

The three moons had passed. The young man left the forest and set out for the palace. As he approached it, he began singing and playing his *chirimía*. The princess was in her chamber looking out her window, sadly. Then she saw him approach and heard his music. To the princess, his tune sounded more beautiful than that of any bird. Dashing from her room, she ran joyfully to welcome him, knowing this was the man whom she would marry.

Prove It

What details in the story show how the young man responded to a challenge he faced?

The Open and Shut Case

by L.J. Sands

"Achoo!" Willa sneezed. She had been up in the dusty attic looking through boxes of old toys and books. She felt like an explorer searching for treasure in a distant country.

She was just about to go back down when a gleam of light from across the room caught her eye. She went over and found a small leather case. Something was painted across the top. In bright red and gold, as if on a banner, were the words *Viola and the Violettes*.

Willa undid the latches and slowly lifted the lid. There *was* a treasure inside! In a sunken bed of purple velvet, shaped to fit its curves, rested a silver saxophone. "Momma!" Willa shouted. "Look what I found!"

Her mother came upstairs. "What is it, honey?"

"It's a saxophone," Willa replied. "But who was Viola, and who were the Violettes?"

Mom shook her head in wonder. "I don't have any idea. Maybe Dad knows."

But Willa's father didn't have a clue.

"Come on!" said Willa. "There's a *saxophone* in our attic! It must have some connection to us."

Mom and Dad looked through old family photo albums to see if anyone with a saxophone showed up. As they searched for photos, Willa brought over the family laptop and typed "Viola and the Violettes" into the search engine. Nothing came up. Then she tried using the phrase "band + saxophone." This led her to the world of the Big Bands of the 1940s.

"Hey, look at this," said Willa. "These bands didn't play electric guitars. They look like small orchestras." Willa found a video link and opened it. "Here's a whole row of people playing saxophones and trombones. But these musicians are all men."

"Except for the two singers," said Mom.

Looking further, Willa and Mom learned that during World War II, most young men joined the armed forces to fight. In their place, all-girl bands entertained the country. These bands traveled around by bus and train. They even performed on the radio.

Zoom In

What mystery does Willa want to solve? What details in the story helped you answer?

Many women who before the war might have been criticized for going on the road were now praised for helping to keep people's spirits up during the war.

"So there were women who played in bands after all," said Willa.

"You must be on the right track," said Mom.

But by four o'clock, no one had any real answers.

Willa stared out the window at the passing cars. "Don't get discouraged," her dad said.

"That's it!" Willa shouted, leaping up from the table. She grabbed a pencil and paper and ran back up to the attic. Half an hour later, she sat her parents down in front of the computer and typed the name "Laurie Jo Stein" into the search engine.

Bingo! Up popped dozens of listings for that name, plus references to the Violettes. There were photos and a home movie and a few scratchy recordings.

"That's my grandmother!" Mom exclaimed. "She lived right in this house long ago. The house remained in our family, and we never cleaned out the attic completely. The saxophone must be hers. I always knew there was something she'd given up early in her life, but I never thought it was a music career! How did you figure it out?"

"Well," explained Willa, "I noticed the case only because of a tiny flicker of light. Downstairs, when the sun glinted off the chrome of a passing car, I realized that there must be something metal on the case. When I ran back upstairs to check, I found a brass nameplate from the manufacturer on the case. It said *McMann's Musical Instruments, Kokomo, Indiana.* I looked them up online and found they were still in business. So I called, and they told me where to find the serial number on the saxophone, and I did, and they matched it to a receipt for a Laurie Jo Stein, who bought it on *May 20, 1935!*"

Mom put her arm around Willa. "Great detective work, honey."

"Yes, indeed," said Dad. "In fact, we could say that you closed the case."

Prove It

Which sources helped Willa track down the answer to the mystery?

May 12

What I Read

- Sound travels through the air in waves.

- Sound travels through other things, too.

- Sound goes through some materials easily.

- Some materials **muffle**, or soften, **sound waves.**

May 13

What I Wonder

- What materials can sound travel through easily?

- What materials muffle sound?

What I Will Do

- I will use my radio to play music.

- I will find out how different materials affect how loud it sounds.

Materials

- Small radio

- Foam pillows

- Wool blankets

- Wooden table

May 15

What I Did

First, I listened to how the noise sounded when it traveled through air. It was loud.

Second, I put my radio under a pile of foam pillows. I could hardly hear the music. The music was muffled.

Next, I wrapped the radio in wool blankets. I put my ear against the blankets. The sound was very muffled.

Finally, I put the radio on a wooden table. I put my ear against the table. The sound was clear.

Zoom In

What steps did the boy take in his experiment?

May 16

What I Found Out

What Sound Traveled Through	How Radio Sounded
air	loud
foam	muffled
wool	very muffled
wood	clear

Summary

The air and wood had almost no effect on the sound waves from the radio. The foam pillows and wool caused the sound waves to be muffled.

The next time my sister plays her radio too loudly, I'm putting wool blankets and foam pillows over my head to muffle the sound!

Prove It

What do you learn about the results from the chart?

Learn the Words

percussion instruments
wind instruments
string instruments
brass instruments
pitch
reflect
detect
echo

- Read the words on the list.
- Read the dialogue.
- Find the words.

How will we arrange the instruments on the stage?

The **wind instruments** should be right behind the singers.

I hope the **percussion instruments** are at the other end, or they will drown out my voice.

1. You Are the Actor
Speaking and Listening

Work with a partner. Ask your partner questions about any vocabulary words you don't understand. Then take turns reading the dialogue in the picture. Use your best acting voice. Try to make the dialogue come alive.

2. Sound Hunt
Graphic Organizer

Think about things that make a noise—animals, machines, doors. Think about the pitch of the noise. Is it a high squeak or a deep, low sound? Make a chart. Name each thing or animal that makes the sound. Share your list with the class.

What's the Pitch?	
High	a cat
Low	a truck

3. Design an Orchestra
Listening and Speaking

Work with a partner. List three percussion instruments and other items that make good percussion sounds. (This includes things you can tap on or strike.) Together, they will make a percussion orchestra. Share your list with the class.

4. You Are the Author
Writing

What musical instrument do you want to learn? Write a paragraph. Name and describe the instrument. Explain why you like that instrument. Or, you can tell about an instrument you are already learning. Explain what you like about this instrument. Show your paragraph to your partner.

Animals Use Sound

by Susan M. Guthrie

Have you ever wondered how a bat locates its food at night, or why a rabbit needs such big ears? The answer is sound. Animals use sound to help them in many ways. Their survival often depends on it.

Dolphins

Ocean water is sometimes hard to see through. Dolphins need to find their way through the water safely in order to find food. They also need to avoid their enemies or other dangers. They use sound to help them find food and stay safe.

Dolphins make clicking sounds or send out creaking vibrations that have a high pitch. The sounds **reflect**, or **echo**, off objects in the water. Returning echoes tell the dolphins the location of the underwater objects. This process is called echolocation.

Click! Click! Click!

Oooohmmm...

Whales

Like dolphins, whales use echolocation for hunting food and navigating underwater. They create sounds through air spaces in their head. By moving air between these spaces, they produce different sounds, such as whistles, clicks, groans, or other kinds of noises. When the whales send out these sounds, they are able to tell a lot about their underwater surroundings by the type of sound that echoes back. For example, they can identify what kind of animals are around, how deep the water is, or what obstacles are nearby.

Some kinds of whales produce sounds that can only be called songs. These songs are among the most complex sound patterns created by non-human creatures. Humpback whales and blue whales are among the types of whales that create songs. No one yet knows what whales are communicating to one another through their songs.

Bats

Most bats are active at night. They use echolocation to help them fly safely and not bump into trees or other objects in their path. It is also what helps them to find their food, mainly insects.

Bats have excellent hearing and big ears that are constantly moving. The ears can **detect** and amplify even the buzz of a bug. To catch a bug, the bat sends out high-pitched squeaks that are too high for humans to hear. The bat listens for the sound to reflect back to them. Bats can tell from the echoes what sort of object is hit. So when the squeaks hit the bug, the sound echoes, or bounces, back to the bat. Then the bat can fly to the right place to snatch the bug for a tasty snack!

Screech

Screech

Rabbits

Not all animal sounds have a high pitch. Some rabbits warn others of danger with low-pitched thumps, or stomping, of their hind legs.

Thumping works hand-in-hand with rabbits' large ears to keep them safe.

A rabbit's ears move either together or one at a time to pick up the thumping sounds from other rabbits. In fact, the large ears can catch sound waves coming from any direction.

Thump!

Thump!

Elephants

Elephants also make low-pitched sounds to communicate with other elephants. Some are so low-pitched the human ear cannot detect them, but they are powerful to the elephant's enormous ears. Elephants can hear one another from more than 2½ miles away!

Scientists call the elephants' low-pitched sounds infrasounds. Some believe the elephants can make these sounds because they have extremely long vocal cords.

Though some of their sounds are low-pitched, other sounds that elephants make are easily heard by humans. Elephants will grumble, scream, groan, rumble, squeal, or make trumpet calls, which is their most common sound. The sound they make depends on what message the animals want to pass along to others. It may be a call for help during an enemy attack or when a family member is lost. It could be a signal to gather the herd to travel to a different location. It might be to show anger toward another elephant. Whatever the sound, the other elephants get the message.

Prove It

What are two reasons animals use sound?

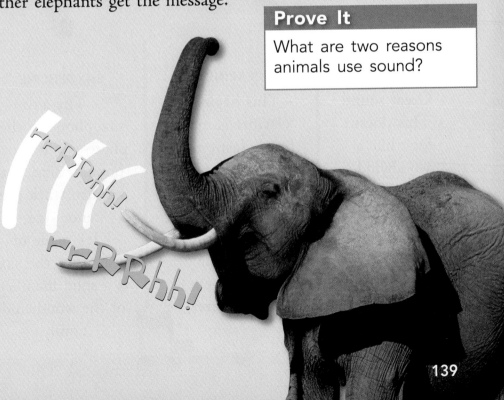

HOME | ABOUT US | SHIPPING | SALE | CONTACT

SCHOOL BAND
INSTRUMENTS

CLICK INSTRUMENT FOR PRICING

WOODWINDS

FLUTE
- Great sound
- This doesn't look like a woodwind because it's made of metal, but it is! The flute is traditionally a must-have for school bands.

CLARINET
- This beginner's clarinet is made from plastic resin with nickel-plated keys.
- Comes with a supply of reeds. Buy your replacement reeds here!

SAXOPHONE
- The alto saxophone in the photo is our most popular size, but we also stock the tenor size.
- It's made of brass, but the sax is a solid member of the woodwind family.

BRASS

↓

TRUMPET

- One of the oldest musical instruments, its bright sound improves the music of any band or orchestra.
- It can be used to play all kinds of music, including jazz.

CORNET

- Rich sound
- Favorite brass instrument for school bands

PERCUSSION

↓

DRUMS

- We have drums of all kinds, including drum sets, snare drums, and bass drums for marching bands, and kettledrums for orchestras.

TRIANGLE

- Every school band needs one!
- Its vibrations produce the loveliest high-pitched tones.

STRINGS

↓

VIOLIN

- Maple and spruce are two precious woods used to make violins.
- Its classic shape helps create an incredible sound.

VIOLA

- The viola, too, is made from quality wood.
- Beautiful sound

MORE GREAT VALUES!

Retell "The Loveliest Song of All"

> ℹ️ When you retell a story, you tell only the most important events. Tell the events in order. Using words such as *first, next, after,* and *finally* can help listeners understand the order of events. You can also show how the main character changes through the story.

"The Loveliest Song of All" is a folktale. Review the story on pages 118–123. Look at the pictures on page 143. They show the story's events in order.

■ **First Row of Pictures:** What is the princess like at the beginning? What happens first?

■ **Second Row of Pictures:** What happens after that?

■ **Last Row of Pictures:** What happens next? What is the princess like at the end?

Use the pictures on page 143 to retell the folktale to your partner. As you tell about each event, point to the correct picture. Use complete sentences.

> **Words you might use in your retelling:**
>
> | wind instrument | pitch | note |
> | detect | volume | beat |

princess is sad

king tries
to help

princess meets
man

man wants to
marry her

Spirit of the
Woods helps

princess is happy

Dig Deeper

Look Back

You have now read two mysteries, "The Open and Shut Case" in this unit and "Fighting Words" in Unit 2. On a sheet of paper, write the answers to these questions.

1. In each story, what mystery is the main character trying to solve?

2. What object in each story leads the main character to the mystery?

3. What does the past have to do with each story?

4. How does the main character use clues or research?

5. What other characters help the main character?

Talk About It

Some sound words actually sound like the sounds they make. Here are some:

| boom | crash | drip | tweet | click |
| beep | splash | sprinkle | babble | splat |

With your classmates, come up with a living thing, an object, or an action that might make each sound.

Conversation

 You can use words to show how you feel. You can also express something you need. You can begin sentences with the words *I feel* or *I need*.

Talk to a partner. One of you will be person A.
The other will be person B.

Person A

Person B

Ask how your partner feels.

Reply. Ask how your partner feels.

Reply. Ask if your partner needs anything.

Reply. Ask what your partner needs.

Reply. Thank your partner.

Reply. (What do you say when someone thanks you?)

IN THE DEEP

The BIG Question

How are plants and animals affected by their environment?

☐ What are some things that scientists discovered about the deep seas?

☐ How do sea animals find their food?

☐ What is life like in a tide pool?

What life forms can be found in the sea?

1. What can you find in an ocean?

An ocean has…

- ☐ animals with many arms.

- ☐ animals with shells.

- ☐ animals that glow in the dark.

- ☐ plants of different shapes and colors.

2. What is probably true of life forms near the bottom of the sea?

Deep-sea life forms most likely…

- ☐ don't get any sunlight.

- ☐ don't need to breathe air.

- ☐ need some way to get food.

- ☐ look very different from land animals.

3. **What marine life forms do you want to see?**

I want to see...

- ☐ a brightly colored fish from a coral reef.
- ☐ a transparent jellyfish.
- ☐ a whale.
- ☐ a starfish.

4. **Have you ever seen an ocean?**

I have seen...

- ☐ the Atlantic Ocean.
- ☐ the Pacific Ocean.
- ☐ the Indian Ocean.
- ☐ the Arctic Ocean.

Say **more!**

environment
organism
zone
depth
trench
coral
marine
exist

Theme Vocabulary

The easiest way to remember the meaning of a new word is to use it. As you discuss deep-sea animals and plants, use these vocabulary words. Use them when you read and write about life in the deep sea, too.

Read the word.
Look at the picture.
Use the word in a sentence.

environment

organism

zone

depth

trench

coral

marine

exist

Which Picture?

Look at the vocabulary cards. Choose one picture. Don't tell anyone what it is! Describe the picture. See if your partner can guess which picture you chose.

Taking Care of Lola

Mom **Rasheed** **Lola** **Mrs. Garcia**

1. Sure, Mrs. Garcia. Rasheed is home. He can take care of Lola.

   I love my mom, even when she asks me to do something that I have a gut feeling will be hard.

2. Mrs. Garcia is coming with Lola. Can you keep an eye on Lola while they're here?

3. OK, Mom. I just hope she won't give me a hard time.

4. Yikes! This kid has trouble written all over her!

   She's a nice kid. I'm sure you'll like her.

11) **Formal/Informal Language** "To hit the roof" is an expression that means "to get very upset or angry." Would you be more likely to say this when talking to friends, or to your teacher?

14 Expressions When Rasheed thinks, "And not a moment too soon!" What does he mean?

OCEANS OF THE WORLD

NORTH AMERICA

ATLANTIC OCEAN

28,374 feet
8,648 meters

SOUTH AMERICA

PACIFIC OCEAN

Key

deepest part of ocean

ARCTIC
OCEAN

ASIA

EUROPE

PACIFIC
OCEAN

36,198 feet
11,033 meters

AFRICA

INDIAN
OCEAN

23,812 feet
7,258 meters

AUSTRALIA

SOUTHERN OCEAN

ANTARCTICA

157

Opinion

Save Our Sea Turtles!

by Rufaro Okonjo

Sea turtles are one of Earth's oldest creatures. These ancient ocean dwellers have been around for 150 million years—since before the time of the dinosaurs. Sea turtles live in all the world's oceans except for the Arctic. Their shells are streamlined for swimming through the water.

There are seven species of sea turtles. The smallest, the Kemp's Ridley, weighs from 80 to 100 pounds. The largest, the leatherback, can weigh over 2,000 pounds.

All species are either endangered or threatened. About 1 in 1,000 baby sea turtles will make it to adulthood. The biggest threats are caused by humans. They include poachers, fishers' nets and hooks, the destruction of their nesting beaches, pollution, and plastic debris in the ocean. Also, climate change causes rising sea levels, which can destroy the turtles' nesting beaches and food sources.

We should do all we can to help save these ancient creatures from extinction!

If you live in an area where there are sea turtles, here is a "to do list":

1. Turn out any lights from the beach. Artificial lighting confuses hatchlings and leads them in the wrong direction.
2. Reduce the garbage you produce and clean up trash on the beach. Sea turtles can become tangled in trash or even eat it.
3. Avoid nesting places where there are hatching turtles. You don't want to trample the hatchlings as they head to the water.
4. Volunteer! Organize a clean-up day with your friends and clear the beach of litter.
5. Donate money to one of the save the sea turtle organizations or have your class "adopt" a sea turtle.
6. Talk to friends and family about what they can do to help these creatures survive!

from
Robinson Crusoe

a story by Daniel Defoe
retold by Judy Rosenbaum

What would you do if you found yourself shipwrecked all alone on an island? That's what happened to Robinson Crusoe. This book is a work of fiction. However, it was based on the life of a real person, Alexander Selkirk.

When I awoke, the weather was clear and the storm was over. The sea was calmer than it had been the day before. I was surprised to see that the wrecked ship had been lifted off the sandbar and brought closer to the shore. It seemed to be less than a mile from where I stood, and it was almost upright. I wanted to get to it. Maybe there were supplies on the ship that I could use.

I climbed down from my "apartment" in the tree. By about noon, the sea had become very calm. The tide had gone out far enough that I could walk out partway to the ship. I swam the rest of the way.

The ship lay high out of the water. This put the deck very far up from sea level. I had to swim around the ship twice before I saw a way to board her. Finally, I saw a rope hanging down. I used it to climb up and in.

I searched around to see what was dry and what the salty seawater had ruined. I was able to fill my pockets with biscuits. I ate some as I explored the ship. Now all I needed was a boat to carry things from the ship to the island! But there was no such boat to be found. Well, it was a waste of time to sit and wish for what could not be. Whatever I needed, I would have to make myself. So I looked around for loose pieces of wood from the ship itself. I threw the pieces overboard. Then I went down over the ship's side. I tied the wood pieces securely together with the rope and laid planks crosswise over them. I found I could walk easily on this raft. However, I could see that it wouldn't bear any great weight. With a saw, I cut one of the masts into three lengths. I added these to my raft. It took a lot of work! But I needed those supplies.

My raft was now strong enough. I thought
carefully about what to load onto it. I got three
chests. I filled them with bread, dry rice, cheeses,
dried meat, and some dried corn. I also took along
whatever useful clothes I could find. After a long
search, I found the chest of the ship's carpenter.
The tools inside were very useful prizes to me,
more valuable than a shipload of gold. I also took
some rifles and bullets, and two rusty old swords.

The raft was now well-loaded. I began to wonder
how I would get it to shore. I had only a broken
oar to move and steer the raft. I had three pieces of
luck, though: a calm sea, a rising tide, and a light
wind blowing toward shore. I ended up only a short
way from where I had put out to sea.

Here I almost had a second shipwreck. If this had happened, I think it would have broken my heart. Knowing nothing of the coast, I had let one end of my raft run aground. Since the raft was not aground on the other end, it tilted downward toward the water. I feared that all the supplies would fall off the raft and be lost. I did my best, by setting my back against the chests, to keep them in place. But I couldn't risk moving from that position to push off from the sand with the oar. So I stayed like that for nearly half an hour!

Then the rising water lifted my raft so that it was level once more. I was able to steer it to the mouth of a little river. After much effort, I got my raft onto land.

Crusoe returns to the ship eleven times in the next thirteen days. Each time, he takes useful things from the ship. One day, the wind begins to rise. Another storm is on its way. He makes one last swim to the ship. Then the storm blows in. It breaks the ship completely apart.

Prove It

What details show that Crusoe is able to deal with tough moments in life?

Octopus Food Fight

by Patricia J. Murphy

Lines are drawn on the ocean floor.
Who'll win less?
Who'll win more?
Day or night, any time is right
For an octopus food fight!

Dances of color,
Flashes of light,
Black streams of ink
Float far out of sight
In an octopus food fight!

Tangled tentacles are
Grabbing . . .
Squeezing . . .
Fighting to eat . . .
A super-sized treat.

Yes, that's right . . .
Not everyone wins
In an octopus food fight!

from
"We Waves"

by August Strindberg

We, we waves
That are rocking the winds
To rest—
Green cradles, we waves!

Wet are we, and salty;
Leap like flames of fire—
Wet flames are we; . . .

We, we waves,
That are rocking the winds
To rest!

Life Deep Down

by Susan Buckley

In 1977, Dr. Robert Ballard traveled 8,000 feet below the **surface** of the Pacific Ocean. Dr. Ballard is a **marine** scientist, a scientist who studies the ocean. He was in a special submarine called *Alvin*. *Alvin* can go down to a **depth** of three miles below the ocean surface.

The scientists had gone to a special spot in the Pacific Ocean. They were looking for areas of very hot water on the ocean floor. Hot seawater comes from vents, or cracks, in the ocean floor. Underwater volcanoes heat the water to about 700°.

At the underwater vents, scientists were shocked by what they saw. Thousands of feet away from sunlight, there was life! Until then, scientists did not think life could **exist** without sunlight.

In fact, there were many **life forms** in the deep-sea **environment**. These life forms were creatures that could **survive** without any sunlight at all.

Going Up the Food Chain

The most surprising find at the vents was **bacteria**, the smallest living **organisms**. Some of the bacteria make their food from chemicals in the deep, hot water. These bacteria are the first level in what is called the food chain.

Small animals are the next level in the food chain. They feed on the bacteria. At the top of the food chain are larger animals like octopuses and giant squid. They eat the smaller life forms.

Giant tubeworms live around the vents. The tubeworms have no stomachs or mouths, but they eat tiny bacteria. In turn, shrimps and crabs eat the tubeworms.

Food Chain Facts

In most known food chains, plants are the first link. Plants use sunlight to make their own food. Then animals eat the plants. The food chain around the deep hydrothermal vents is different. There, bacteria are the first link, and they make their food from chemicals, not sunlight.

Adapting to Survive

The organisms in the deep ocean are not like life forms near the surface. They have adapted to the extreme conditions in their dark world. In other words, they have changed to live in that environment.

No sunlight reaches that far down. Some deep-sea fish make their own light. Their bodies glow! The glow serves two purposes. It can help the fish attract prey to eat. It also can confuse predators who want to eat it. Some anglerfish have tiny glowing bits in their fins, for example. The fins look like small creatures that other fish like to eat. When those fish get too close to the anglerfish, then they become the meal!

Because there is so little light, some deep-sea creatures have no eyes at all. Other creatures have extra-sharp eyes that can see the glow made by the creatures around them.

Some deep-sea squid are **transparent**. You can see through them! Octopuses and squid have another trick. They squirt ink to prevent predators from finding them. One kind of squid even squirts glowing ink.

The transparent giant squid lives at depths of over 1,000 feet. It grows to a length of at least 60 feet!

Adapting to Slow Down

Scientists are still learning about the deep ocean world. They have many questions that they cannot answer yet. For example, they believe that the life forms in the deep ocean live at a slower pace.

Animals in sunlight often chase their prey long distances. The predator needs to be very speedy to catch the prey. In the dark, things are different. A creature cannot see far enough to follow its prey. So it does not need to move so quickly.

Deep-sea creatures grow more slowly than others. They also live very, very long lives. Scientists believe that an orange roughy fish can live as long as 125 years! A deep-sea rockfish might live up to 100 years.

Scientists have not figured out the reasons for this slower life. A more limited food supply may be one reason.

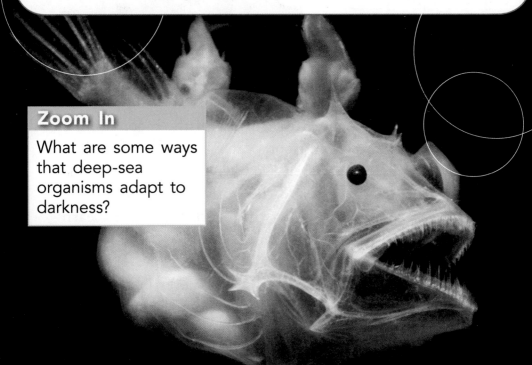

Zoom In

What are some ways that deep-sea organisms adapt to darkness?

Deep Sea Fact
The Mariana **Trench**, in the Pacific Ocean, is the deepest part of any ocean on Earth. The trench is 36,198 feet deep. That's almost 7 miles below the surface of the ocean!

Explorers of the Deep

Seawater covers about 70 percent of Earth's surface. Almost none of the ocean floor has been explored. It is simply too deep. We have mapped the surface of the moon more completely than the ocean floor.

This is changing, however. Now we have better technology and can travel deeper. Around the world, scientists are studying the deep ocean. What they learn helps them learn about Earth and how it was formed.

The deepest parts of the ocean are full of life. There are more mysterious life forms than scientists ever imagined. The amazing way these creatures have adapted to living without sunlight shows that living creatures find a way to survive in even the most unfriendly habitats. So studying the deep ocean environment helps us understand how life might exist on planets other than Earth.

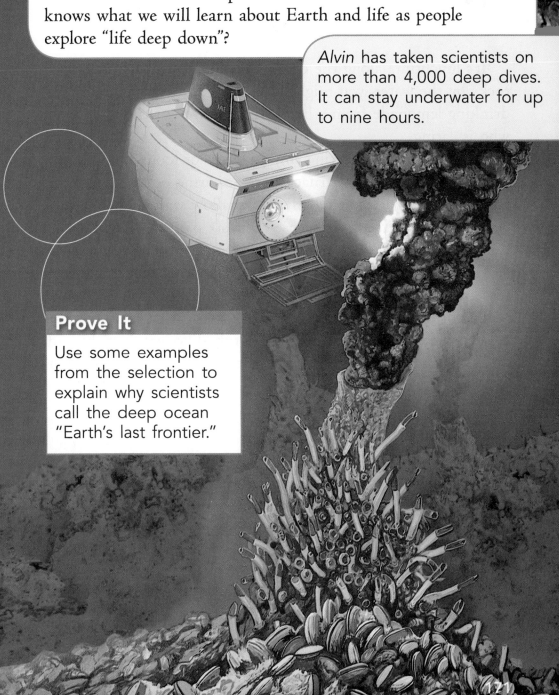

The submarine *Alvin* still takes marine explorers down to the depths of the ocean. Meanwhile, scientists are creating new vehicles. Some are run by robots. Others work by remote control from ships on the surface.

Scientists call the deep ocean "Earth's last frontier." Who knows what we will learn about Earth and life as people explore "life deep down"?

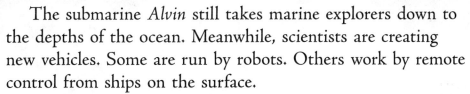

Alvin has taken scientists on more than 4,000 deep dives. It can stay underwater for up to nine hours.

Prove It

Use some examples from the selection to explain why scientists call the deep ocean "Earth's last frontier."

Eating in the Zone

by Malika Rand

It's lunchtime along the ocean coastline. Sitting on the rocks by the water, you might be holding a sandwich and drinking lemonade from a bottle. But you're not the only one who is eating.

The barnacles are eating tiny particles of food—and they're eating with their feet! Barnacles are a marine organism with a hard shell. Barnacles usually live in shallow water, where they cling to hard surfaces. They use their six pairs of feet like feathers to filter food from the sea.

Some limpets are using their long ribbon-shaped tongues to scrape food off the rocks. Limpets are a kind of sea snail.

Starfish (also called sea stars) are also meat eaters. They eat mostly shellfish. With its many tiny, tube-like feet, it grabs and holds the shell of its prey. Next it uses its "arms" to crack open the shell.

barnacles

This is all happening in and near tide pools. Tide pools are pools of **salt water** that fill and empty with the tides.

The level of the ocean rises and falls either once or twice a day on almost every coast in the world. These movements are called tides. When the sea level rises, water rushes toward the shore. High tide is the time of highest sea level. Then the sea level falls. The time of lowest level is low tide.

You can divide the coast into four tidal **zones**. Each zone is described by the amount of time it is under water.

The Splash and Spray Zone: Above the high tide line, it's mostly dry. It gets moisture from salt water ocean spray.

The High Tide Zone: The top of this zone is under water about 10 percent of the time.

The Middle Tide Zone: This area is under water about half the time. Living things here must be adapted for wet and dry conditions.

The Low Tide Zone: This zone is under water 90 percent of the time.

limpet

hermit crab

Who Eats What?

All the creatures in a tide pool must find their food there. They are all part of a food chain. A food chain is not a real chain that you can see or hold. It's a way of describing how living things are linked by what they eat. For example, in a tide pool, organisms called algae grow on rocks. A limpet eats the algae. A sea star eats the limpet. Then a seagull eats the sea star. The algae, limpet, sea star, and seagull are linked together in a food chain.

The creatures that live near each other can't all eat the same thing. If they did, there wouldn't be enough to go around. Instead, each animal has adapted to get the nutrients (foods) it needs. Part of the fight for survival is finding a place on the food chain that is not too crowded. That way, an animal has a better chance of getting enough to eat.

sea urchin

Plants and algae are the first link in almost every food chain. They use sunlight to make their own food.

The next link in the chain is the animals that eat only plants and algae. These are called herbivores.

Carnivores are next. They eat meat in the form of the herbivores. Some carnivores also eat other carnivores. A seagull will eat a starfish, which eats mussels and limpets.

Some creatures eat both plants and animals. These are omnivores. For example, a sea urchin eats algae, but sometimes it eats mussels.

Within their groups, most animals eat a few different foods. What they eat depends on what they can find. In any environment, there may be hundreds of kinds of living things. Each group of animals has a few things they eat and a few things that eat them. So the food chain can get tangled!

seagull

sea mussels

Copying Nature

A starfish can grow back an "arm" when one breaks off. If humans could regrow body parts, it would change medicine forever. Scientists are trying to figure out exactly how starfish are able to do this.

starfish

Prove It

What are some details from the text that support the idea that tide pool animals are part of a food chain?

SWIMMING IN THE FOREST

by Susan Buckley

There are no footpaths in this forest and no signs. There are no forest rangers, either. As you look around, you see no bears, no chipmunks, no birds. Instead, giant **seaweed** plants **surround** you, swinging gently with the ocean surge. As far as you can see, the ocean is filled with plants that reach down more than 100 feet below the surface of the Pacific Ocean.

Brightly colored fish swim in and out of the dense, tall green seaweed. What's that enormous brown shape resting on the surface? It's a three-ton elephant seal. It is hiding in the forest so sharks can't find it. And there's a sea otter floating on its back, having a sea urchin lunch.

Where in the world are you? You're in a kelp forest off the coast of California.

fronds

These bladders are filled with gas, so they float, holding up the top of the kelp.

Kelp Forests

Kelp forests stretch along the coastline of North America from Alaska to Baja California. Two different kinds of kelp make up the forests: giant kelp and bull kelp.

All kelp plants begin on rocks. Instead of roots that go deep into the earth, kelp anchors itself on the rock with what is called a holdfast. From the holdfast, the plant begins to grow upward. Like all plants, kelp makes its energy from the sun. So it grows toward the surface sunlight. It takes nutrients from the surrounding water. Its stalk is called a stipe. Attached to the stipe are fronds, which are like leaves.

stipe

Kelp Forest Facts

- Kelp forests can be found in cool waters around the world from Korea to Australia. Because the plants need sunlight, they grow in clear, shallow waters along coastlines.

- Giant kelp can grow to be more than 100 feet long, from the holdfast to the surface. It grows faster and taller than any other marine plant. Sometimes it grows as much as two feet a day!

holdfast

sea otters

Sea otters use tools! They use rocks to open the shells of the sea urchins they eat.

baby fish

A Forest Home

Like any forest, a kelp forest is the home to a wide range of plants and animals. Kelp forests give food and shelter to more than 1,000 different species.

Kelp forests are like rain forests. The thick vegetation at the top of the forest makes a canopy. As you read on page 176, animals such as seals and sea otters find safety from predators there. Of course, sharks, killer whales, and other predators know the prey is there. Often, they cruise by the kelp forest. They're looking for an easy meal when a seal or sea lion leaves the forest.

Sea otters raise their young in the kelp canopy. The thick kelp forest is like a playpen for baby otters. When their mothers leave to hunt for food, they keep the babies safe by tying them with a kelp frond! Then the adults glide through the canopy. They graze for food such as crabs or snails or urchins.

spiny lobster

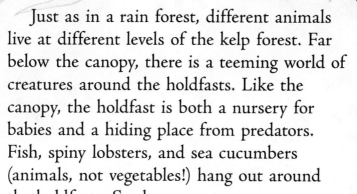

Just as in a rain forest, different animals live at different levels of the kelp forest. Far below the canopy, there is a teeming world of creatures around the holdfasts. Like the canopy, the holdfast is both a nursery for babies and a hiding place from predators. Fish, spiny lobsters, and sea cucumbers (animals, not vegetables!) hang out around the holdfasts. So do octopuses and moray eels. Divers have counted about 180 different organisms on one holdfast!

Zoom In

What details from the selection show that kelp forests are like rain forests?

A Green Highway?

Some scientists believe that giant kelp forests may have stretched across the Pacific from Japan to the Americas. Historians believe that some of the first people to come to the Americas came by boat from Asia. Traveling across the kelp forests may have helped them make this journey. The forests were filled with things to eat. And the dense plant life would have blocked the force of the waves. This would make it easier for travelers in open boats.

moray
eel

octopus

sea
cucumber

Kelp Forests in Danger

For as long as there have been kelp forests, there have been natural threats. Mainly, these come from storms. Wind and giant waves rip the kelp from its holdfasts. But kelp grows quickly, and in a short time the forests grow back.

Today, however, kelp is threatened in more serious ways. One threat is water pollution. Another great danger comes from warmer water. When the water temperature is just a few degrees too high, kelp forests die off. In recent years our entire planet has grown warmer. This puts kelp at risk.

Overfishing is another problem. As humans eat more and more fish, the fishing industry uses techniques that harm the entire marine world. The fishing boats' giant nets don't catch just fish. Other kinds of sea creatures also get caught in the nets. These creatures are often just thrown away.

Kelp forests are beautiful, wild places that shelter more than 1,000 species of plants and animals. Saving kelp forests is part of saving our planet.

Did you know . . . ?

Kelp is used in products from ice cream to toothpaste to car tires to shampoo. Part of the kelp plant is something called align. It keeps liquids thick and smooth.

Seeing the Kelp Forests

The best way to see a kelp forest is to dive right into it. This means using scuba equipment. *Scuba* stands for "self-contained underwater breathing apparatus." Two French divers, Jacques Cousteau and Emile Gagnan, invented this equipment. Scuba gear includes a tank of air that the diver wears.

Licensed to Dive

There is a lot more to scuba diving than putting on a tank. Before you dive, you need to be certified by professionals. People 15 years old and older take Open Water diving courses. These courses teach the information, skills, and rules for diving in a lake or an ocean.

Many dive organizations will certify Junior Open Water Divers between 10 and 14 years old. Junior divers take the regular course to learn how to scuba dive safely. Junior divers can dive in open water only with a certified adult.

Prove It

What details tell you how widespread kelp forests are in the world?

Learn the Words

transparent
bacteria
life form
survive
seaweed
surround
salt water
surface

- Read the words on the list.
- Read the dialogue.
- Find the words.

Did you know there are undersea volcanoes? They erupt under the **surface** of the ocean.

Deep in the sea, amazing things **surround** you.

BOUT SKUNKS

A skunk's smell helps it **survive**.

JUDGE

That is how they scare off predators.

1. Interview from the Field
Listening and Speaking

Pretend you are a reporter. Plan an interview with one of the people in the picture. You could choose a student, a judge, or one of the other adults. Write five questions you would ask that person. Share your questions with your partner.

2. Can You See Through It?
Graphic Organizer

What things are transparent? What things are not transparent? Think of items you use or see every day. Classify each item. Write it in the correct row in the chart. Share your chart with the class.

Transparent or Not?	
Transparent	
Not Transparent	

3. Write a Poem
Writing

Many people have written poems about the sea. Now it's your turn. You can write about how the ocean looks or about marine life forms. You can even write as if you are a sea animal! You can use the poem in this unit, "Octopus Food Fight," as a model. Share your poem with your partner.

4. Make a List
Vocabulary

Work with a partner. Name as many life forms as you can. They can live on land or in water. Think big, and think small! Remember that plants are also life forms. Share your list with the class.

COME BACK, SALMON

by Marlena Diaz

WASHINGTON

Columbia River

Four main kinds of salmon are born in the Columbia River: Chinook, Coho, sockeye, and chum.

For millions of years, the salmon of the Columbia River followed the same pattern. Adult salmon would swim from the Pacific Ocean up the Columbia River. They swam right back to where they were born. The fish laid their eggs and, in a short time, died. Months later the young salmon would swim out to the ocean. After a few years in the ocean, the cycle would begin again. The adults would make their way back to the very spot where they had been born.

Different kinds of salmon had slightly different patterns. Some spent only a year in the ocean before returning home. Others spent up to seven years. Some young salmon spent only a short time in the river. Others spent a year or more there before heading to the ocean.

How did the salmon know how to go home after years in the ocean? No one knows exactly how they made this amazing journey. For a long time, scientists thought a sense of smell helped the fish navigate. A new theory says that salmon learned their home "address" based on the Earth's magnetic field.

Along the Columbia River, however, the salmon's life cycle has been changed. In the 1930s the United States began building dams to control the river. Today there are many dams.

Today, salmon can't swim freely up the river. When a dam blocks the river, the salmon are pushed over to the side, where there are concrete waterways. The fish jump from one step to another to travel up the river. Many die in the process.

Numbers tell a tragic story for the salmon. In the 1800s there were between 10 million and 16 million salmon in the Columbia River. Today only about 200,000 to 300,000 wild salmon swim up and down the river.

Several kinds of wild salmon are endangered today. If changes are not made, they could disappear completely. But it is not easy to know what to do. The Grand Coulee Dam completely blocks salmon from their trip up the river. Yet this dam is one of the largest sources of electrical power in the world. So far, no one has figured out how to balance the needs of people and the needs of the salmon.

For salmon, getting upstream by the side of a dam is like jumping up a ladder.

Our Colorful Oceans

by Charles Tanaka

Put on your mask and snorkel and take a look. You are on the Great Barrier Reef off the coast of Australia. There is color everywhere. Hundreds of different kinds of fish swim around you. In just a small area of water, there can be 200 different kinds of fish. There are tiny orange-and-white clownfish. A gorgeous angelfish glides by. Its blue and pale green body looks as if it's covered in jewels. You might even see butterfly fish, with black spots on bodies that look like wings. Down in the sea grass is a green turtle.

The **coral** is colorful, too. As you float along, you see a field of brown staghorn coral on one side. Round shapes of pale brain coral sit next to the waving tentacles of a group of mushroom corals. Don't touch that reddish fire coral, though. It will give you a sting!

The rainbow of color is everywhere. On the sand below you, a giant clam opens its shell. The lining looks like a huge pair of turquoise lips. There's a red hermit crab crawling out of a borrowed shell. The octopus has the right idea in this colorful world. It changes color whenever it wants to!

Coral Facts

Just what is coral, anyway? It may look like a rock, but it's really a meat-eating animal. A reef is made up of millions of coral polyps. The word *polyp* comes from a Greek word that means "many feet." A coral polyp is a tiny animal. It can be as small as the head of a pin or as big as a pencil eraser. It is a very simple animal with a stomach and a mouth. Around the mouth are many tiny tentacles that look like feet. The polyp uses those "feet" to capture its food.

Polpys build a structure around themselves out of limestone from the water. A coral reef is made out of the limestone formations of many polyps.

Coral polyps can divide themselves to create new polyps. Also, once a year they release eggs into the ocean. They hatch into new polyps. In just a few years, one polyp can increase to about 25,000 polyps.

The Great Barrier Reef is one of the most amazing and colorful places on Earth. It stretches 1,250 miles along the northeastern coast of Australia. It is made up of about 3,000 smaller reefs. The Great Barrier Reef is the largest structure on Earth made by living creatures.

Retell "Life Deep Down"

 When you retell a selection, you give only the important ideas and details. This helps readers understand what the selection is mostly about.

"Life Deep Down" is an informational article. It gives facts about life forms at the deepest parts of the Pacific Ocean. Review the selection on pages 166–171. Look at the pictures on page 189.

■ First Picture: What is the importance of *Alvin?* How did it help scientists learn about deep-sea life?

■ Second, Third, Fourth, and Fifth Pictures: What main points does the selection make about each of these kinds of life forms?

Use the pictures on page 189 to retell the selection to your partner. As you talk about each idea or fact, point to the correct picture. Use complete sentences.

Words you might use in your retelling:

environment	depth	exist
life form	survive	salt water

life in the deep sea

Alvin

tubeworms

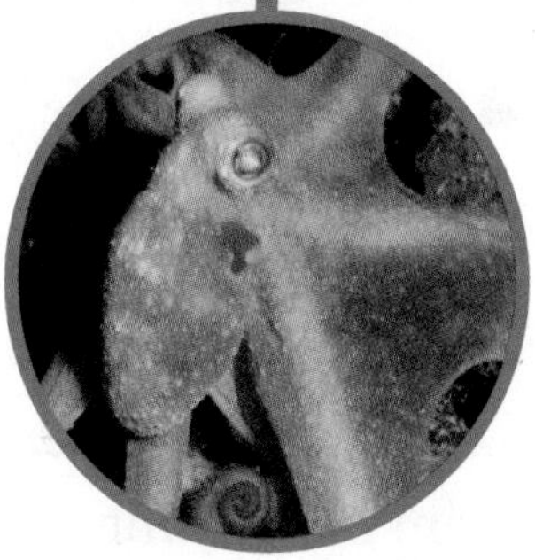

octopus

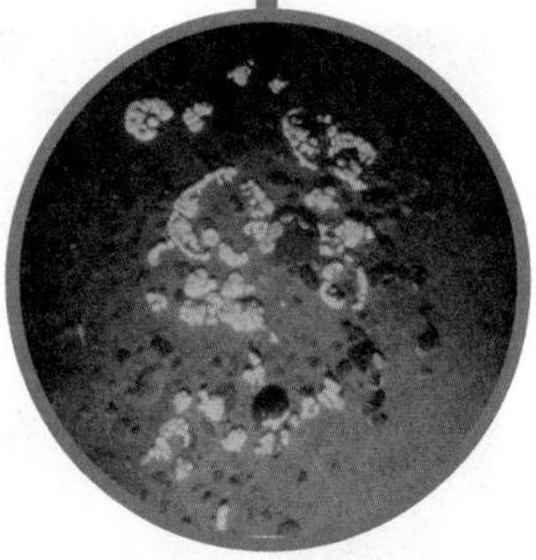

bacteria

squid

Dig Deeper

Look Back

Work with a partner. Suppose you are both preparing a TV program about the ocean. Which five facts about the ocean and its plants and animals would you most want to share with the audience? Here are some possibilities:

- a fact about kelp forests

- a fact about living things at the bottom of the ocean

- a fact about the submarine *Alvin*

- a fact about tide pools

- a fact about a coral reef

Discuss with your partner what facts you would choose. On a sheet of paper, write the facts and where you found them in the unit.

Talk About It

If you could dive down into the sea, which animal would you most like to see?

Share your choice with your classmates.

Do you agree with your classmates? Why or why not?

If not, what can you say to convince others to agree with you? What could get you to agree with others?

Conversation

It's fun to discuss what you like and dislike. Use words, but show your feelings in your face, too. Remember to be polite if you disagree with someone else.

Talk to a partner. One of you will be person A. The other will be person B.

Person A

Person B

Tell about something you like.

Agree or disagree. Tell about something you like.

Agree or disagree. Tell about something you dislike.

Agree or disagree. Tell about something you dislike.

Agree or disagree. Ask about something else your partner likes.

Answer your partner.

A Growing Nation

The **BIG** Question

How did our country grow and develop?

☐ What were some reasons that people traveled to the American West?

☐ How did early settlers in the U.S. travel long distances?

☐ What was it like to settle somewhere far from home?

Let's Talk

What was life like for pioneers of the past? What is life like for pioneers today?

1. **What makes someone a pioneer?**

   A pioneer can be…

   ☐ one of the first people to do something new.

   ☐ someone who helps to start new settlements.

   ☐ someone who faces new challenges without much help.

   ☐ a person in the past, or a person of today.

2. **How would you go on a long journey if you couldn't use cars, buses, or jets?**

   I could travel by…

   ☐ foot.

   ☐ horseback.

   ☐ steamboat.

   ☐ wagon.

3. **What hardships do people face in a new land?**

   Often, people in a new land…

   ☐ don't know the language.

   ☐ must find or build shelter.

   ☐ face harsh weather.

   ☐ deal with new kinds of dangers.

4. **How can you learn about the history of a place?**

   You can…

   ☐ visit historic places.

   ☐ read about people who lived there long ago.

   ☐ ask a guide or an expert.

Say **more!**

Learn the Words

westward
expansion

frontier

wagon

expedition

journey

caravan

pioneer

hardship

Theme Vocabulary

ⓘ The easiest way to remember the meaning of a new word is to use it. As you discuss our growing country, use these vocabulary words. Use them when you read and write about our growing country, too.

Read the word.
Look at the picture.
Use the word in a sentence.

westward expansion

frontier

wagon

expedition

journey

caravan

pioneer

hardship

Match the Pictures

Look at the pictures on the vocabulary cards. Choose two pictures that go together. Tell why you think the pictures go together.

Basketball Stories

2 Formal/Informal Language When Juan says that he "felt like a fish out of water," he means that he "felt strange, or uncomfortable." How could he say "I felt like a fish out of water" in a more formal way?

After the game...

OK kid, let's call it a day.

You made some slick moves.

At least they noticed me. But if I was with my guys, I'd be calling the shots. I was their go-to guy.

9

10

The next day, I went back just to see what was going on.

Duc's not here again.

Hey, Juan, want to play?

11

You're open, Juan. Go for it!

12

10 **Expressions** "To call the shots" is an informal expression. What do you think it means?

200

13 **Formal/Informal Language** "Right on the money" is another way to say "exactly right." Is this expression formal language or informal language?

201

PEOPLE ON THE MOVE

by Caroline Dempsey

Long, long ago there were no people in the Americas. Then, more than 13,000 years ago, people began to populate the two continents. Over thousands of years, these first Americans were on the move. They spread out across North America and South America. They went to live in the mountains and on the plains, in forests and in deserts. They built shelters out of wood, animal skins, and sun-baked clay.

About 500 years ago, new people arrived in the Americas from Europe and Africa. They, too, were on the move. They first settled on the Atlantic coast. But from the time the United States became a nation, **pioneers** like Daniel Boone were leading people to the West.

The 1800s were the time when **westward expansion** was at its peak. "Go west and grow with the country," a leading newspaper urged.

Pioneers traveled west in wagons about 4 feet wide and 10 feet long. Each wagon was filled with all of the possessions a family needed for a new life.

There was good farmland in Oregon Country and gold in California. "Oregon fever" and "gold fever" were in the air, and people rushed west. They traveled from their homes in **wagons** and **stagecoaches** and on trains. They took **steamboats** and ferries across the Missouri and Ohio rivers.

Cities such as Independence, Missouri, were the starting points of the long and hard **journey**. There, pioneers joined others heading in the same direction. They formed **caravans**, groups of 30 or more wagons that would travel together.

When the first wagon trains crossed the Missouri River, they reached lands that were already home to thousands of American Indians. The westward expansion of the United States was an exciting story for the pioneers. But often it was a story of loss for the first Americans.

Report

Survival!

by Roberto Ortíz

In the early 1600s, two groups of people sailed to the American continent from England. One group landed in Virginia and started the Jamestown settlement. The other group landed in Massachusetts and formed the Massachusetts Bay Colony.

Both groups were looking for new opportunities in America. Both took huge risks to make the voyage. Both discovered that they were not prepared for the difficulties ahead, which included starvation and disease.

Jamestown was settled mostly by people who wanted to get rich quick and go back to England. They were not very religious. Their community life and family life didn't mean much to them. They often fought with each other.

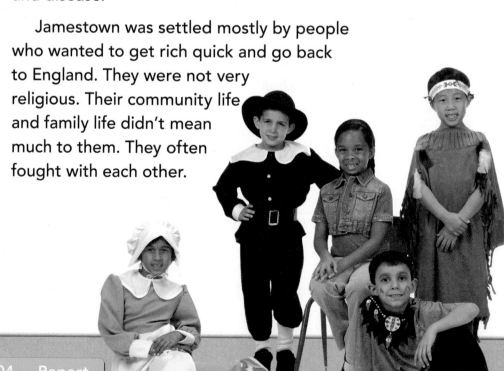

The Massachusetts Bay Colony was founded by Puritans, who were very religious. Puritans believed in hard work and religious devotion. They allowed no entertainment. Puritans punished their members who broke the rules.

The settlers of the Massachusetts Bay Colony knew that they needed friendly relations with the native population. The Wampanoag assisted them.

By contrast, the Jamestown settlers did not want to get along with the native population in their area. They were called the Powhatan. The settlers wanted to dominate them.

Which settlement do you think survived? Jamestown, with its greed and fighting, or the Massachusetts Bay Colony?

Exploring the West

by Susan Buckley

It was 1803, and President Thomas Jefferson had just doubled the size of the United States. The country had bought the Louisiana Territory from France. The United States now stretched far west beyond the Mississippi River. However, no one in the United States knew what that land was like or who lived on it. Jefferson asked his secretary, Meriwether Lewis, to head a journey of exploration. Lewis asked his friend William Clark to join him on the **historic expedition**.

With a group of about 45 men, Lewis and Clark set out from St. Louis, Missouri, in May 1804. They were headed to the new **frontier** of the United States.

Jefferson wanted to learn about the geography of the new territory. He wanted to know whether there was a water route reaching all the way to the Pacific coast. Water travel was much easier than overland travel in those days. Jefferson also wanted to communicate with and learn about the Native Americans who lived in the area.

By August 1804, Lewis and Clark made contact with the Oto and Missouri peoples, hunters and farmers along the Missouri River. Later, two new members joined the group. They were Sacagawea, a Shoshone woman, and her French Canadian husband. They would act as **guides** and interpreters.

As the expedition traveled west, Sacagawea became more and more valuable. This area was the homeland of her people, the Shoshone. When Lewis and Clark needed horses, Sacagawea translated the explorers' request to her people. The Shoshone gave them the horses they needed.

After crossing the Rockies, the group met the Nez Perce people, who helped them make new canoes to carry them down the Columbia River. After wintering with the Clatsop people at the Pacific coast, the expedition set out for home. They reached St. Louis in September 1806.

Telling the Story

by Angela Castillo

How do we know so much about the journey of Lewis and Clark? Both of these explorers kept journals. So did some of the other members. In words and drawings, they described what they saw, what they did, whom they met.

The journal entries you see here are based on what the explorers recorded.

September 10, 1805

Most of the men went out hunting today. In the evening one of the hunters returned with three men on horseback. They are of the Flathead people. The men were upset because men from the Snake people had stolen many of their horses. The Flathead men were chasing the thieves.

Sacagawea helped us understand what the men wanted to tell us. She does not speak their language, but she understands the hand signals they used.

Two of the Flathead men left to find the thieves. But one stayed with us, offering to be a guide across the mountains.

Each American Indian group has its own language. Before English was a common language, using hand signals, or signing, was a way different groups communicated with one another.

September 20, 1805

Our group met three Nez Perce boys today. They ran into the grass when they saw us. We walked over to them and gave them some small gifts. Then we met a man, who took us to the house of the lodge of the chief.

We were hungry and the adults gave us food. They gave us berries, dried salmon, and roots that taste like onions. They also gave us a small piece of buffalo meat.

We visited two villages and stayed the night. We did not feel well, however, as we had eaten too much.

TALL TALES AND BIG HEROES

by Michael Kwan

Did you ever hear the story about Pecos Bill, the cowboy? They say he could ride a mountain lion and that he used a rattlesnake as a whip.

And what about Paul Bunyan? They say that this logger could eat 50 pancakes in a minute. He and his giant blue ox, Babe, dug the Grand Canyon when Paul dragged his ax behind him.

Of course, you can't really believe these stories. In fact, they are called "tall tales." In a tall tale, facts are greatly exaggerated to create a funny story like Paul Bunyan eating pancakes or a thrilling one like this tall tale in song form about the strongman railroad worker John Henry.

It's interesting that many of the heroes of tall tales were people doing specific jobs—cowboy, logger, railroad worker. These tall tales show how important ordinary working people were to Americans.

John Henry

adapted by Elaine Kule

John Henry said to his boss,
"I am just a man,
But before I let your drill beat me down,
I'll die with my hammer in my hand."

John Henry held his hammer.
Beside the steam drill he did stand.
He beat that steam drill three inches down
And died with his hammer in his hand.

And every time that train goes by,
They say, "There lies a hard working man.
There lies a hard working man."

Prove It

How does the song show that John Henry is a tall tale character? What line gives the best clue?

Journey on the Royal Road

by Katacha Diaz

Catalina Sosaya opened her sleepy eyes and pushed back her blanket. She didn't like getting up so early. But today her family was starting on a long journey. They would leave their home near Tucson in New Spain to go to a new home in Alta California. It was October 1775.

Catalina opened the secret place in the bottom of her trunk. Carefully, she hid her gold locket and other prized items there. She'd heard stories about thieves attacking caravans going north. She wasn't taking any chances.

Outside, the Sosaya family's wagon was packed with their possessions. Catalina sat in the back with Mamá and Abuelita. Her older brother, Gonzalo, sat up front with Papá.

Catalina could see people and animals everywhere. Mamá said that 240 men, women, and children were traveling together. And there were so many animals—about 1,000 horses and mules and cows. Tomasa, the Sosayas' milk cow, was tied behind the wagon. Abuelita's chicken coops were fastened to the sides.

Catalina and her family were pioneers. They were part of a great expedition led by Juan Bautista de Anza. The king of Spain, Charles III, had ordered Commander de Anza to take settlers to Alta California. King Charles wanted to be sure California was settled by Spaniards.

For months the caravan traveled north on El Camino Real, the Royal Road. It was named for an earlier Spanish king, Philip II. Spaniards had been traveling El Camino Real for almost 100 years. They built **missions** and presidios, or forts, along the coast. At the missions, Spanish priests taught their religion to the Native Americans.

All day long the caravan traveled on the dusty trail. Every night they stopped to make **camp**. Catalina helped Mamá milk Tomasa while Abuelita collected eggs for their evening meal. Sometimes there were dust storms, and as winter came, the temperature dropped. But those were not the only **hardships** they faced.

One night the cow, Tomasa, got loose and wandered off. The Sosayas **depended** on Tomasa for milk. Catalina knew that if Papá couldn't find her, they would have to leave her behind. Papá searched near the campsite. Then Catalina saw Senor Romero leading a cow toward the family's wagon.

"Isn't this your cow?" asked Senor Romero. He was holding Tomasa's rope. "We found her with our cattle."

When Mamá thanked Senor Romero, he said, "We are alone in the wilderness. We must depend on one another."

Catalina gave Senor Romero a grateful smile. It seemed that even before her family reached their new home, they had found people who would be good neighbors in Alta California.

Zoom In

Why was an expedition sent to California? Support your answer with evidence.

It took the pioneers six hard months to reach the presidio at Monterey. Monterey was foggy and cold, so different from the sunny warm weather the Sosayas had left behind.

The presidio was built for soldiers, not settlers. Catalina wasn't sure she was going to like life on the frontier! She and Abuelita sometimes went to the mission at Carmel, though. Father Junípero Serra had founded the mission a few years earlier.

Soon Commander de Anza took some of the men and traveled further north to San Francisco Bay. But the Sosayas and most of the other settlers stayed near Monterey.

In time, the Sosayas built a new home. They were happy to end their adventures on El Camino Real. And they were excited to begin a new life on the frontier.

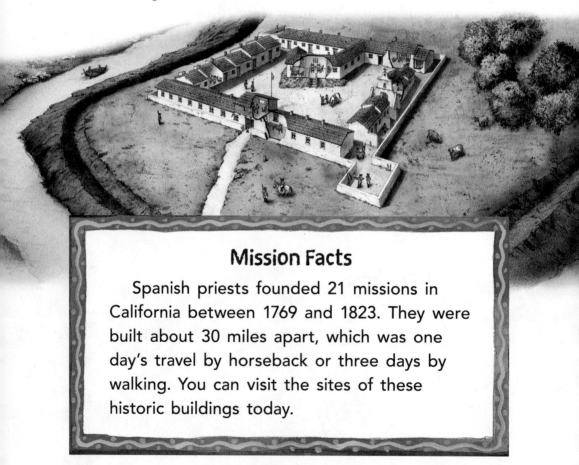

Mission Facts

Spanish priests founded 21 missions in California between 1769 and 1823. They were built about 30 miles apart, which was one day's travel by horseback or three days by walking. You can visit the sites of these historic buildings today.

Prove It

What evidence shows that the Sosayas' trip was very hard?

The Californias

In the Spanish empire, there was a province called Las Californias, or "The Californias." It was made up of Alta California (Upper California) and Baja California (Lower California). From 1804 on, these two pieces of land were **governed** as separate territories. In time, Alta California became the U.S. state of California. Baja California still exists. It is part of Mexico.

GET READY ☞ WE'RE HEADING WEST!

by Alba Mendez

Are you planning to head west to Oregon Territory? Don't go before you read this!

SO YOU WANT TO BE AN OVERLANDER

Are you sure about this? Being an overlander means you're going to travel by land all the way to Oregon. Your journey will take as long as six months and cover about 2,000 miles. You'll cross a wide, treeless, grassy plain. Then you'll reach a wall of stone and snow thousands of feet high—the Rocky Mountains. Only by crossing them can you reach your new home on the far frontier.

THE WAY WEST

The pioneers who came before you established a route now called the Oregon Trail. It starts at Independence, Missouri. The trail follows river valleys and winds through passes in the Rocky Mountains. There aren't any actual roads, though. Your bumpy trip will take you over dirt, grass, stones, mud, and the deep grooves left by the wagon wheels of earlier travelers. Are you still interested? Here's how to prepare.

START WITH THE WAGON

The old Conestoga covered wagons that haul freight in the East are too heavy for this trip. You need a "prairie schooner." Some people think these wagons got their name because tall prairie grass ripples like ocean waves. A schooner is a kind of ship. This is not a steamboat, though! It is powered by strong animals, not steam.

This wooden wagon is only about 9 to 11 feet long and 4 feet wide. It's pulled by a team of 4 to 6 oxen or 10 to 12 mules. It's covered in canvas. Make sure to waterproof the canvas cover with wax, grease, or oil.

WHAT TO TAKE WITH YOU

farming and building tools

pots, pans, dishes

a barrel to hold water on the trip

blankets

candles and matches

cloth, sewing tools

plant cuttings and seeds for your farm

a tent for sleeping

140 to 200 pounds of flour per person

40 to 140 pounds of bacon (a meat that doesn't go bad quickly)

30 pounds of hardtack (special long-lasting biscuits)

dried foods: fruit, peas, beans, corn

eggs (packed in cornmeal so they won't break)

219

MEET UP IN INDEPENDENCE

Try to plan your trip ahead. The best time to start from Independence is in the spring. This will get you through the mountains before snowfall blocks the passes. Don't leave too early in the year, though. Wait until the prairie grass grows, because that's the food source for your livestock.

In addition to the animals pulling your wagon, you may be bringing a horse or two and some cows for milk. You might have your family dog, too, for protection!

At your starting point, you'll join with 30 or more other families to form a wagon train. You might be traveling with friends with whom you have planned this trip. Or you may meet up with new companions in Independence. Whatever you do, you cannot make this trip on your own.

Before you set out, you'll elect a leader or hire a guide. This person makes important decisions for the wagon train, such as how long to travel each day.

ON THE TRAIL

On the trail, the day starts before sunrise. You have a lot to do before you get going. You must prepare breakfast and load the wagons. You need to gather the milk cows (and the dogs, too) and then hitch up your team.

You'll probably travel from 12 to 20 miles each day. After you stop for the night, form the wagons in a circle. This helps you fence in all the animals so they don't wander off.

Here's one last hint for your trip. You're making history, so be sure to keep a journal. People in the years to come will want to know what it was like to cross a continent. Have a great trip and a wonderful new life!

Prove It

What is one reason that people needed to plan ahead for a westward trip by covered wagon? What is your evidence?

CALIFORNIA, HERE WE COME!

by Nikolai Borovsky

It was a cool California morning in January 1848, and James Marshall was supervising the building of a sawmill. Walking along the American River near Sacramento, Marshall saw something shiny at the bottom of a ditch. As he told it later, "I reached my hand down and picked it up; it made my heart thump, for I was certain it was gold."

Marshall's guess was correct. There was gold in the American River. The sawmill's owner, John Sutter, wanted to keep the news to himself. But soon everyone knew about it and rushed to Sutter's Mill. Wild reports of people finding fortunes in gold swiftly spread across the country and around the world.

AN ACCOUNT OF

CALIFORNIA,
AND THE
WONDERFUL GOLD REGIONS.

A New Arrival at the Gold Diggings.

WITH A DESCRIPTION OF
The Different Routes to California;
Information about the Country, and the Ancient and
Modern Discoveries of Gold;
How to Test Precious Metals; Accounts of Gold Hunters;
TOGETHER WITH MUCH OTHER
Useful Reading for those going to California, or having Friends there.
ILLUSTRATED WITH MAPS AND ENGRAVINGS.

BOSTON:
PUBLISHED BY J. B. HALL, 66 CORNHILL.
For Sale at Skinner's Publication Rooms, 60½ Cornhill.

Price, 12½ cents.

In the gold rush of 1849, more than 80,000 people raced to California. They were known as forty-niners. At first, many of the forty-niners found gold easily. It was right on the surface of the riverbeds (the dirt and gravel over which the river flows). But as more and more people arrived, it was harder and harder to find gold. Some of the disappointed forty-niners went back home, but many stayed. They became farmers or found other ways to earn a living.

All of these new people changed California. Before the gold rush, California was governed by the United States, but it was not yet a state. In 1849, Californians asked to become a state. It became the nation's 31st state in 1850.

Journal *of a* Forty-Niner

This journal tells the story of a young man who journeyed more than 2,000 miles in hope of becoming rich.

ᷔ ᷕ

April 13

Today our steamboat arrived in Independence, Missouri. It has been nine days since we left St. Louis. Father and I have joined with our company to travel west. We've bought our mules, built our wagon, and packed our mining equipment. Soon our group of wagons will depart.

May 15

We've been traveling west for a little over a month now. On the trail today we met a group traveling from Salt Lake back to St. Louis. They told great stories of the gold region, including one about a man who collected $750 worth of gold in one day. They have been traveling for 30 days. My excitement to reach our destination grows.

June 7

Every day there are more and more wagons passing ours. We are all concerned about how slowly we are moving. I wonder whether there will be any gold left by the time we reach California.

June 18

The traveling has become more difficult. We have trouble finding good grass for our mules. The countryside is barren, with just some small trees and sagebrush. Today we reached the place where the California and Oregon trails part. We watched the wagon train ahead of us turn off for Oregon.

July 24

We are crossing a terrible section of desert, 45 miles long. Signs posted along the trail warn about the hardships. We travel at night to avoid the heat. The sand is so deep that we can barely move the wagons through it. We threw out extra supplies to lighten the wagons' loads.

August 6

Today we arrived at a difficult mountain, but at least we are past the desert. At the base of the mountain were all sorts of goods that others had abandoned—gold-washing pans, picks, shovels, and large quantities of food. With great difficulty, we moved our wagons up the rocky path.

August 14

Today, at long last, we arrived at Sutter's Mill. The trip to get here was so difficult, and the dangers we faced so great, that I think no amount of gold could convince me to do it again.

We saw a group of small log buildings and also met some of our company who had ridden ahead. They showed us the gold they had found already. It was about half an ounce each per day. The gold pieces are about the size of corn kernels.

August 16

We sold the wagon and mules for $700 and set up our tent in the miners' camp. Food and other goods here all sell for very high prices.

August 20

We found gold today! I found a small piece and some flakes, or "gold dust." Father found some tiny pieces. We were digging in the streambed, washing away the sand and gravel, and hoping for bits of gold to be left in the pans. The excitement of finding that first piece of gold was wonderful!

September 8

The camps and the streambeds get more crowded every day as more men come here to join the search for gold. Although we have found some gold, the expenses are much higher than at home. Some of our company can't afford to stay here. They have gone to San Francisco hoping to find work. We have decided to keep trying for a few more months. But unless we meet with great success, we may return home.

Prove It

What elements of this selection tell you that it is a journal entry?

guide
govern
mission
historic
steamboat
depend
stagecoach
camp

- Read the words on the list.
- Read the dialogue.
- Find the words.

I'm glad we hired a **guide** to lead our wagon train.

We can **depend** on him to find the safest route.

1. Interview
Listening and Speaking

Suppose your partner arrived at the town shown in the picture above. The year is 1850. Ask your partner five questions about his or her life. Then change roles. Have your partner ask you five questions.

2. Take a Survey
Graphic Organizer

Survey several classmates. Ask how they would have traveled long ago. Tally their votes. Share your findings with your partner.

How Would You Travel?	
I would go by...	Number of Votes
steamboat	
stagecoach	
covered wagon	

3. You Are the Writer
Writing

What historic place have you visited? Tell about your visit. Or, describe a historic place you want to visit. Write a paragraph. Tell what is important about that place. You can look back through the unit for ideas. Share your paragraph with your partner.

4. Two Different Versions
Listening and Speaking

Suppose you are a guide and you are showing visitors the historic town in the picture above. It looks the same today. Tell your partner how the town was built. Tell who built it. Then listen to your partner tell how the town was built. How is each person's version alike? How is it different?

Get It There Fast—or *Faster*

by Peter Chen

Suppose you are in St. Louis, Missouri, and you want to get in touch with a friend in San Francisco, California. Today you can text your friend, make a phone call, or send an e-mail. But in the 1800s, you would have to write a letter and send it by boat. This would take months.

You could send a letter by stagecoach or train in the East. You could even send a telegram. But no stagecoach routes, railroad lines, or telegraph wires reached all the way across the continent. Then, in 1857, a stagecoach service began between St. Louis and San Francisco. The trip was over 2,000 miles long and took about 25 days. This was still much faster than a trip by boat.

The stagecoaches traveled about 8 miles per hour, 60 to 70 miles per day.

In 1860, a new mail service called the Pony Express began. It carried mail from Missouri to California in just 10 days. For 18 months, bold young Pony Express riders rode so fast that they had to change horses every 10 to 15 miles. Every 75 to 100 miles, a new rider took over while the other rested. It took 75 horses to make the full trip.

In 1861, telegraph wires were finally laid all the way to the west coast. Suddenly you could send a message across the country in moments. That was the end of the Pony Express.

But what if you still wanted to send an actual letter? Railroads were the answer. Begun in 1863, the first transcontinental railroad spanned the continent by 1869. You could send your letter from New York to San Francisco in about a week. In 1869, that seemed like instant communication!

Prove It

What details show how coast-to-coast communication speeded up through the mid-1800s?

FROM SEA TO

by Thomas Lee

1783: The new United States of America was made up of just 13 states. All of them lay along or near the Atlantic coast.

1848: In just 65 years, the young nation would stretch 3,000 miles across the continent to the Pacific. How did this happen?

The Louisiana Purchase, 1803

The United States doubled in size when Thomas Jefferson purchased the Louisiana Territory from France. All or part of 14 states were formed from the land. These include Arkansas, Missouri, Iowa, Oklahoma, Kansas, Nebraska, Minnesota, North Dakota, South Dakota, New Mexico, Montana, Wyoming, Colorado, and Louisiana.

Florida, 1819

Spain signed a treaty with the United States, giving Florida to the U.S. in exchange for U.S. claims in Texas. A few years earlier, Spain had given up claims to lands along the Gulf of Mexico that became part of Mississippi and Alabama.

SHINING SEA

Texas, 1845

In 1836, after spending centuries as part of New Spain and then of Mexico, Texas won the right to govern itself. It became the independent Republic of Texas. Nine years later, the republic became the 28th state in the United States.

Oregon Country, 1846

To avoid a war, Great Britain and the United States agreed to divide the Oregon Country between Canada and the United States. The states of Oregon, Washington, and Idaho would be formed from the territory.

Mexican Cession, 1848

At the end of the Mexican War, Mexico gave up the territories that would become the states of California, Nevada, Utah, and parts of Colorado, Arizona, and New Mexico.

And then we were 50 . . .

By 1912, the last western territories became states, and the nation had 48 states. When Alaska and Hawaii were added in 1959, we became a nation of 50 states.

Retell "Journey on the Royal Road"

 When you retell a story, you tell only the most important events. Tell the events in order. Using words such as *first, then, later,* and *finally* will help listeners understand the order of events.

"Journey on the Royal Road" is historical fiction. The story is based on real events, but the people are made up. Review the story on pages 212–217. Look at the timeline and pictures on page 235.

■ First Picture: What does the timeline show about the start of the journey?

■ Second, Third, and Fourth Pictures: What story events took place during the journey?

■ Fifth Picture: What story events took place in April?

Use the pictures on page 235 to retell the selection to your partner. As you talk about each idea or fact, point to the correct picture. Use complete sentences.

Words you might use in your retelling:		
frontier	wagon	journey
caravan	pioneer	hardship

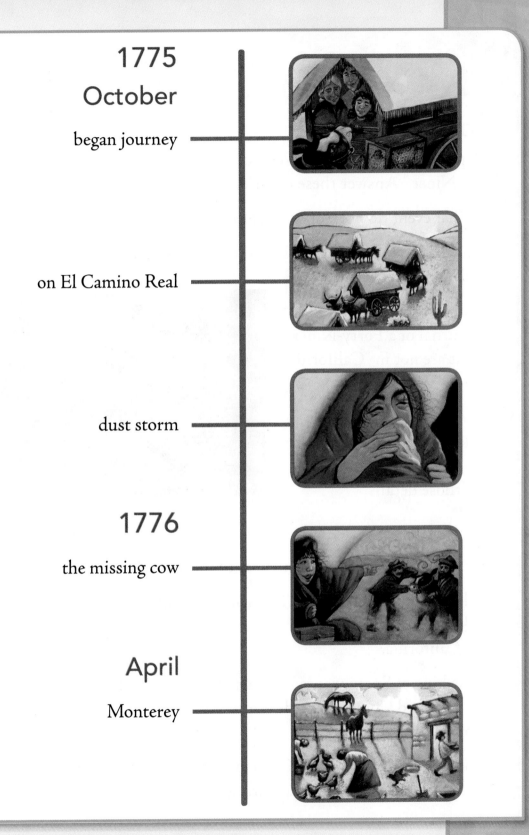

1775
October
began journey

on El Camino Real

dust storm

1776
the missing cow

April
Monterey

Dig Deeper

Look Back

Compare "California, Here We Come!" and "Journal of a Forty-Niner." Answer these questions on a sheet of paper.

1. What event do both of these selections tell about?

2. In what two different ways do these two selections tell about the event?

3. What are two facts in the "Journal of a Forty-Niner" that are <u>not</u> in "California, Here We Come!"?

4. Which selection gives more details about travel to California? Give two of those details.

Talk About It

How can we combine two sentences to make one?

> The king of Spain wanted Spanish settlers in California. He asked Commander de Anza to lead a group to California.

> The king of Spain wanted Spanish settlers in California, so he asked Commander de Anza to lead a group to California.

Work with your classmates. Come up with other pairs of sentences that can be joined with *so*.

Conversation

> ℹ️ To speak formally, use polite words. Speak carefully, and use a serious tone of voice. You might show less feeling than normal.

Talk to a partner. One of you will be person A. The other will be person B.

Person A

Person B

Use **formal** language. Tell your partner about an event.

Reply in formal language. Ask how your partner feels about the event.

Reply in formal language.

Use **informal** language to tell about the same event.

Reply in informal language. Ask how your partner feels about the event.

Reply in informal language.

237

Technology Matters

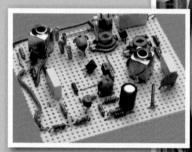

The **BIG** Question

How has technology changed our lives?

☐ What inventions have made people's lives easier?

☐ How have computers and other technology changed since you were born?

☐ How did the invention of trains change people's lives?

What kinds of technology do we use every day?

1. **What kinds of technology help people communicate?**

   People can communicate by...

   ☐ talking on a cell phone.

   ☐ sending an e-mail.

   ☐ leaving a voice mail message.

   ☐ sending a text message.

2. **What inventions have made travel better?**

   Traveling is easier today because we have...

   ☐ jets.

   ☐ cars.

   ☐ super-fast trains.

   ☐ highways.

3. What do you wish you had invented?

I wish I had invented…

- ☐ the airplane.
- ☐ the computer.
- ☐ the air conditioner.
- ☐ the skateboard.

4. How can technology improve people's health?

Technology can help us to…

- ☐ make snacks with less fat, salt, and sugar.
- ☐ develop better medicines.
- ☐ build safer cars.
- ☐ clean up air pollution.

Say **more!**

Learn the Words

communicate
technology
innovation
satellite
telegraph
invention
device
model

Theme Vocabulary

 The easiest way to remember the meaning of a new word is to use it. As you discuss technology, use these vocabulary words. Use them when you read and write about technology, too.

Read the word.
Look at the picture.
Use the word in a sentence.

communicate

technology

innovation

satellite

telegraph

invention

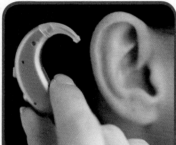

device

model

How Do You Feel?

Look at the vocabulary cards. Choose one picture and tell how it makes you feel.

WHOSE PHONE?

 Juanita

 Natsumi

1. Whoever lost this cell phone must be flipping out! How can I give it back?

2. I lost my cell phone. How am I going to get it back? I'll be in the doghouse if I don't find it.

3. "Mom" is one of the names on the phone. I'll try to give her a ring.

MOM
555 5016
UNCLE DAVE
555 4555
AUNT SAL
555 5533

4. "Mom" is not picking up. Well, I guess she isn't at home.

2) Formal/Informal Language How could you say "I'll be in the doghouse" in more formal language?

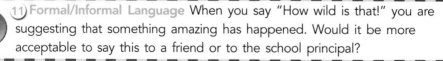

11) **Formal/Informal Language** When you say "How wild is that!" you are suggesting that something amazing has happened. Would it be more acceptable to say this to a friend or to the school principal?

246

13

Hi. I'm Natsumi.

Hi. I'm Juanita.

14

This is your phone.

Thanks so much. I owe you big time.

15

EAT HERE

Let's grab a bite at Big Jim's. This one is on me.

15 **Expressions** "This one is on me" is an informal way to say "I'll pay for this."

THE MANY USES OF GPS

by Aldo Castelli

In the past, people used maps to figure out how to get from one place to another. Now, along with maps, people use an electronic **technology** called Global Positioning System, or GPS.

GPS is computer software. It uses **satellites** to gather and send information. It tells where places are. It can also tell travelers how to get from one place to another. It can even tell them when they will arrive based on the speed they are traveling.

GPS is used on ships, on jets, and in cars. It has more uses than just for vehicles, though. The in-car GPS receiver is generally portable. That means you can carry it around with you. The receiver usually has a driving mode and a walking

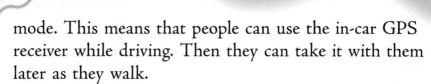

mode. This means that people can use the in-car GPS receiver while driving. Then they can take it with them later as they walk.

For example, a woman drives into a city to visit a museum. Her in-car GPS receiver tells her which roads and streets to take. It tells her where to turn and whether to turn right or left. After reaching the museum, the woman parks her car.

Then she switches the receiver to walking mode and carries it with her. The GPS receiver directs her to the main entrance of the museum. Later, she uses the GPS receiver to find a restaurant.

The smartphones that we use today also have GPS. People can use their smartphones with GPS to get walking directions to the places they want to go.

Prove It

What example does the author give to show how the same person uses two modes of GPS?

Cell Phone Rescue

by Charles Karpiuk

Materials List:	Time Required: 24 hours
■ cell phone	■ vacuum cleaner
■ tap water	■ bag of dry rice
■ towel or t-shirt	

So I'm waiting for the bathtub to fill up for my evening bath when all of a sudden my mom's cell phone slides out of her shirt pocket and falls into the water. *Kerplop.* My mother gasped. She stores her life on that cell phone.

I wanted to help, but I didn't know what to do, so I did a quick **online** search. I typed in the words "**PHONE WATER HELP.**" I clicked on the first one that popped up. I followed these steps:

1. **DO NOT** touch the phone if it's connected to a wall charger. It could kill you. Instead, leave it alone and call for help.

2. If the phone is not connected to a charger, take it out of the water and **TURN IT OFF** as fast as you can. After the phone is **OFF** take the battery out.

3. Dry the phone with a towel or t-shirt. **DO NOT** turn it on even if it seems dry. It's only dry on the outside. There is still water inside.

4. Next, hold a vacuum cleaner over all of the openings on the phone for about half an hour. **DO NOT** let the vacuum cleaner touch the phone. **DO NOT** try and use a hair dryer, oven, or microwave.

5. After that, put all the parts of the phone in a bag of dry rice. Wait about 24 hours. Be patient.

6. Finally, put the battery back in and turn **ON** the phone. If you acted fast enough, the phone should be okay.

7. This works for most electronics. After I read the instructions to my Mom, we did all the steps. The next day, she turned on the phone, and it worked! I'll have to remember this the next time my little sister throws my MP3 player in the toilet.

Playing It Safe on the Web

by Sam Mitschke

Are you playing it safe online? Whenever you log into e-mail, chatrooms, blogs, and other forms of social media, you should play it safe and protect yourself.

What sorts of dangers can you encounter on the Web? You might find yourself talking to someone who sounds friendly. However, the person may not be who he or she seems to be. The person may be trying to learn personal information about you or your family.

There are several things you can do to keep yourself safe on the Web whenever you log on.

1 Avoid Strangers!

Never talk to strangers on the Web. You should **communicate** only with people you know and trust. These include your good friends and family members.

2 Don't Respond!

If anyone online talks about something unkind or uses language that makes you uncomfortable, don't respond. Log off immediately and tell an adult what has happened.

Keep It Safe!

Never give your last name, address, telephone number, or password to anyone you meet online. The person may sound your age and friendly. But the person may be pretending. He or she may want personal information from you. Never give out personal or family information.

We all know that the Internet is a great resource. It can help you do your schoolwork, communicate with friends, play games, and plan activities. It can help you learn about current events.

Still, you should be aware of some of the dangers of using the Web. When you are online, you need to protect yourself from people who may be trying to steal valuable information about you. Follow the rules you just learned so that you can play it safe and make the most of the Web!

Prove It

What details does the author use to show how people can put themselves in danger on the Web?

A History of Computers

Solange Aristide

The first computer in the U.S. that acted the way computers act today was built in 1946. It was called ENIAC. It was used by the U.S. Army. ENIAC did not look like today's computers. It practically filled a room.

One of the next computers was used by the U.S. Air Force as part of our country's defense system. This computer took up the whole floor of an office building.

In 1964, the computer company IBM created a computer called System/360. It was mainly used for scientific projects.

You've probably noticed by now that none of the early computers were personal computers like the ones we use today. The army and large corporations used these early computers. Each one cost millions of dollars.

In 1981, the first personal computer appeared in stores. This computer would look big to you, but at the time, it seemed small. Everything including the monitor, the keyboard, and the printer could fit on the surface of a large desk.

The early 1990s saw the next **innovation**, the laptop. They took up very little space and were light enough to carry.

Early smartphones were very expensive. In 2007, affordable smartphones became available. These **devices** allow you to telephone or text a friend, take photographs and videos, and connect to the Internet.

The tablet is a recent computer innovation. You touch its screen with your finger to make things appear. Many people use tablets to watch videos and news shows. You can also hook up a keyboard to a tablet.

No doubt we will use new and better computer devices in the near future. What do you think they will look like? What do you think they will be able to do?

Prove It

What details show that computers have gotten smaller through the years?

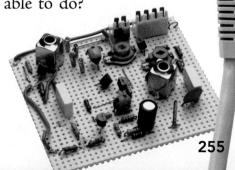

Technology HELPS!

by Lisa Klobuchar

Medicine, science, technology
Have totally changed society.
They let us do things
We hadn't dreamed of before,
Like shopping online
Instead of at the store.

Doctors can cure us when we get ill
With a fancy machine, a shot,
   or a pill.
The universe is not the
   same mysterious place
Since satellites have looked
   deep into space.

Faster, better, smarter—Wow!
Technology separates "then"
   from "now."
But some things stay the same
   through time—
You opened a book to read
   this rhyme.

SKYSCRAPER

By Bobbi Katz

(to honor William Van Alen, skyscraper architect)

With
a frame
of steel
and
a
window
wall
I'll
grow
a
building
strong
and
tall.
Let
it
pierce
the
city
sky.
Clouds don't charge
for
floating by.
Unseen
an
elevator
spine
rises
in
a
steady
line.
I watch this building
and I feel
I hear it
singing
songs in steel.

MARGARET KNIGHT

A LIFETIME OF INVENTIONS!

by Joanne Wachter

While other children were playing, Margaret Knight was inventing toys for her brothers. Throughout her life, she continued to invent many different kinds of things. In fact, she produced about 90 **inventions**. One of these inventions is something that you or a family member probably use almost every day—the flat-bottomed paper bag.

Margaret Knight's Life Begins

Margaret Knight was born in 1838. She was born in the small town of York in the state of Maine. Margaret attended school until she was twelve, when her father died. Then she quit school to work. This was not unusual in 1850.

Like many other young girls of her time, Margaret went to work in a cotton mill. There, she saw a worker get hurt by one of the factory's machines. She quickly set about to invent a part that could make the machine safer. The device stopped the machine if something became stuck in it.

Margaret didn't get a **patent** for her invention, though. Her family had no education and didn't know that people could apply for a patent. A patent is an official government paper saying that an invention is the idea of a specific person. When other people use the invention, they have to pay the patent holder. It's a way to earn money, but the Knight family didn't know anything about this.

Zoom In

What details explain what a patent is and why it is important?

The Famous Paper Bag

By 1868, Margaret and her mother had moved to Massachusetts. There, Margaret got a job at a paper bag factory. At that time, paper bags were shaped like envelopes. These are the shape of paper bags that stores still use for items such as birthday cards. However, flat paper bags would break easily when someone put large, thick objects such as vegetables in them. Margaret had the idea that a paper bag with a flat bottom would be more useful for other kinds of items, such as apples, potatoes, and heads of lettuce.

▲ These drawings show Margaret Knight's ideas for the flat-bottomed bags.

Once she had the idea for the flat-bottomed bag, she knew that she had to figure out a way to make them. She couldn't just make each one of them by hand! That would be too slow. Paying workers to make bags by hand would cost more than Margaret could earn by selling the bags. She needed to invent a bag-making machine.

Inventions in the Age of Factories

Before about 1760, most items were made by hand, one by one. Then people figured out how to build machines that could make a lot of objects in the time it took to make just a few objects by hand. From that time on, many items were made by machines in factories. Factories needed a lot of workers to keep the machines going. The work was hard and sometimes even dangerous. As time went by, inventors figured out ways to make machines safer. Inventors also came up with new items for factories to make and sell.

Margaret set up a workshop where she could **develop** a machine. This machine would have to fold and glue the paper for the bags. First, she made drawings of the machine. Then she made a **model** of the machine out of wood. She started making flat-bottomed paper bags on the wooden model.

She made hundreds of bags on the wooden machine. As she did so, she figured out ways to **improve** her machine. She continued to make changes on the machine until it worked perfectly. Then she ordered an iron version of her machine based on her wooden model.

At last she was ready to apply for a patent. The patent would show that only the inventor has the right to make and sell his or her invention. The patent prevents anyone else from making and selling the item without paying the inventor.

Margaret Knight's bag-making machine looked like this.
▼

Trouble in Court

Margaret was excited about getting a patent for her machine. Before she could get it, though, she ran into a problem. A man named Charles Annan claimed that he had invented the machine. Margaret hired a lawyer and took her problem to court.

During the trial, Annan argued that no woman was capable of inventing a complex machine. Margaret showed the judge her notes, drawings, and models. The judge could see that Margaret had made the machine. She won her case in court and was granted the patent. The machine that could make flat-bottomed paper bags was hers to manufacture and to sell. She was among the first women in the United States to be granted a patent.

The Effects on Business

Margaret's invention had a positive effect on the nation's economy. Before the flat-bottomed paper bag, clerks in stores wrapped items in sheets of paper tied up with string. Some very small, thin items could be slipped into the old-fashioned bags that were shaped like envelopes.

Margaret's machine and the flat-bottomed paper bags it made changed all that for businesses in the United States. Suddenly, grocery stores could quickly pack many different food items in one of the new paper bags. Clothing stores could pack many articles of clothing into a single bag. The clerks in these stores could help customers much more quickly.

Margaret Knight's invention also affected the paper industry in a positive way. Making lots of bags in a short period of time used more and more paper. This increased business at paper mills. In fact, Margaret Knight was voted into the Paper Industry Hall of Fame in 2006.

Another Step Forward for the Paper Bag

Paper bags filled with items can be too large to carry comfortably. In 1912, William Deubner had a grocery store in Minnesota. He noticed that his customers couldn't buy a lot at one time because it was too hard to carry everything out of the store. He used the flat-bottomed bag and glued cord to it. The cord strengthened the bag and could be looped into handles. Deubner patented his invention in 1915. This was the first shopping bag. Paper shopping bags are still used today.

Zoom In

What details explain how Margaret Knight's paper bag was better or more useful than earlier bags?

Recipe for Success

When asked if she found her success surprising, Margaret Knight answered, "I'm not surprised at what I've done." She also said: "As a child, I never cared for things that girls usually do; dolls never possessed any charms for me. The only things I wanted were pieces of wood. I was famous for my kites; and my sleds were the envy of all the boys in town." Clearly, Margaret's early confidence and interests helped her to become a successful inventor.

Over the next forty years, Margaret Knight thought of many other innovations. The U.S. government granted her patents for more than twenty other inventions. Here are a few of her other inventions.

+ a fastener for bathrobes
+ machines for making shoes
+ devices for opening and closing windows

By her death in 1914, Margaret was a very successful inventor. She had invented things that made it easier to manufacture items, such as shoes, on a mass scale. She also invented things that improved the quality of people's lives, such as her window frames for homes. Many of her useful inventions, or variations on them, are still in use today.

Prove It

How does this selection show how inventions can improve people's lives? What details helped you answer?

▲ Today almost all shoes are made by machines.

Working on the
RAILROAD

by Pamela Wright

In the 1860s, most Americans lived east of the Mississippi River, but more and more of them were moving west. At that time, train travel was the fastest, best way to travel, but tracks stretched only from the East Coast to the Midwest. So for six years, between 1863 and 1869, thousands of men worked to build the first transcontinental railroad—a railroad across the continent.

Two competing companies raced to lay the tracks. The Central Pacific Railroad workers started in California. The Union Pacific Railroad workers started in Iowa. After six years, the tracks joined in Utah.

The work of the Central Pacific was the hardest. The railroad had to cross the Sierra Nevada. One American politician said it was like building "a railroad to the Moon." To build the railroad, the Central Pacific hired thousands of Chinese men. This story of Jun Ming could be about any of those workers.

Jun Ming was scared. It was the fall of 1865, and the Central Pacific workers had reached the towering Sierra Nevada. The railroad tracks they were laying could not go over the mountains. They had to go through them! So Jun Ming and his team were digging long, deep tunnels.

At first they had shoveled dirt and hammered stone. They used gunpowder to try to blow up a path for the tracks, but it was all too slow for the bosses. They were clearing only about one foot a day. Then the head of the railroad heard about a new explosive that had been developed. (Now we call it dynamite.) He hoped it would improve progress.

Today it was Jung Ming's turn to carry the dynamite into the tunnel. He was helping to blow up the mountain wall that

was blocking the path of the railroad. It was a dangerous job, so Jun Ming couldn't be careless.

"Be careful!" his friend Luk Sun shouted.

Jun Ming carefully placed the dynamite in the tunnel. He lit the fuse and ran out. There was a huge **explosion**! Jun Ming could feel the **impact**. Rocks and dust flew everywhere. When he looked up, Jun Ming saw that there was a giant hole in the mountain. "Now we can lay the railroad tracks more easily," he thought.

Jun Ming had left his home in China to work for the railroad company. Many of his friends had come to America, too, with thousands of other Chinese men. They called America "Gold Mountain," for they hoped to get rich here.

Instead, they were paid very little for their **labor**. They made only about $30 a month.

Each day of labor was long and hard. Jung Ming got up before sunrise, and he worked on the railroad until long after dark. He dug holes, cleared rocks, shoveled dirt, cut down trees, and built bridges. He laid the railroad ties and iron rails. Every night his back and arms ached, and his legs were sore.

Jun Ming was glad that his friend Luk Sun was with him, though. They had come to Gold Mountain together, and they had planned to go home together. Now the two friends were part of a team of about 15 Chinese workers.

Zoom In

Use details from the selection to explain why Jun Ming was in America.

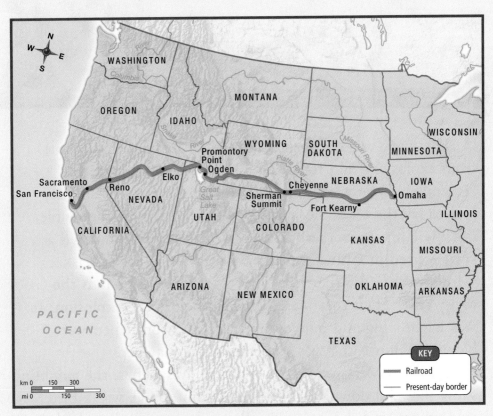

▲ This map shows the route of the Transcontinental Railroad.

271

The work was dangerous. Jun Ming had seen men hurt
from explosions and from the impact of falling rock. He
remembered the work before they began the tunnels. They
had to lay the track along steep cliffs. It seemed impossible,
but the Chinese workers had an idea. They remembered a
system used in China and it worked. Men in small baskets
were lowered over the cliff. They put gunpowder into the
rocky cliff. Then they were lifted up before the explosion. It
was frightening and dangerous work, and some men were
blown up. Jun Ming was glad that task was over!

Now Jun Ming was most afraid of avalanches, the tumbling
snow that slid down from the mountaintops. It was a bitter
cold winter with heavy snows. Recently, two workers had died
when they were buried in an avalanche. Jun Ming was anxious

to begin work inside the tunnel. It was always dark there, but he would be safe from the snow.

In spite of all of the hardships, Jun Ming was glad he had a way to earn money. He had been a poor farmer in China. Even though he earned little here, it was more than he earned in China.

On cold nights in the mountains, Jun Ming dreamed of his home and his family in China. Some of his fellow workers wanted to stay in America after this job was done. Jun Ming was not sure. Before he could think of that, though, he had miles of railroad to build.

By 1868 the Chinese workers like Jun Ming had dug 13 tunnels through the mountains. Once they reached the flatlands of Nevada, their speed improved. They could lay as much as four miles of track every day. Now they worked in larger teams of up to 30 men each.

The workers had another job, too. They set up **telegraph** lines on poles alongside the tracks. The telegraph lines carried news of their progress back to California. The bosses in California were anxious to know the railroad's progress.

Prove It

What details show that Jun Ming's job was dangerous?

Learn the Words

impact
patent
labor
online
improve
medicine
explosion
develop

- Read the words on the list.
- Read the dialogue.
- Find the words.

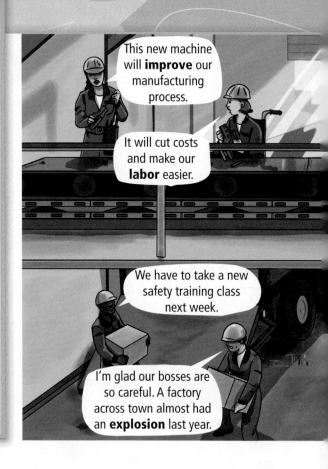

This new machine will **improve** our manufacturing process.

It will cut costs and make our **labor** easier.

We have to take a new safety training class next week.

I'm glad our bosses are so careful. A factory across town almost had an **explosion** last year.

1. Play "Guess Who"
Listening and Speaking

Pick someone in the picture above. Have your partner guess who you chose. Your partner can ask up to five yes-or-no questions first. (It's not fair just to point at each person!) Then change places with your partner.

2. Make a Venn Diagram
Graphic Organizer

You can get information from books. You can also get information online. What is true of books only? What is true of online sources only? What is true of both? Complete a Venn diagram. Show it to your partner.

How Information Sources Help Us

books (both) online

3. Make a Speech
Listening and Speaking

What product or device needs to be improved? Why? Give a speech telling what improvements should be made. Work on your speech with your partner. State your opinions clearly. When you are ready, give your speech to the class.

4. Write a Letter
Writing

Suppose you have invented a new product. You want to take out a patent. Write a letter about your product. Tell what it does. Tell what is different and new about it. Draw a plan of the product. Show your letter and drawing to your partner.

The Train

A Technological Innovation of the 1800s

by Karen Clevidence and Robert McCreight

On a summer day in 1830, America's first locomotive lost a race against a horse! Inventor Peter Cooper wanted to show off his new steam engine. It was called the Tom Thumb, and it could travel at the amazing speed of 18 miles an hour. To test its speed, Cooper raced one train car pulled by the Tom Thumb against another, pulled by a horse. During the race, the steam engine's boiler had problems, so the horse won the race. Soon, however, Americans knew that locomotives were what the nation needed.

By 1860 in the North and the Midwest, railroads linked every city. In the South, they linked farms to ports on rivers and oceans. Railroad companies helped draw Americans to the West. By 1869, the Transcontinental Railroad linked east and west.

Once, the only way to travel across the country was by covered wagon or stagecoach.

Then the steam engine was invented and used to pull trains.

Coal train

Modern high-speed train

Railroads crisscrossed the country, carrying freight and passengers. Over the twentieth century, things changed. Trucks and airplanes now carry most of the freight. Cars and airplanes carry most of the passengers.

For a long time, locomotives were powered by coal. By 1940, diesel fuel had replaced coal. Today, engineers are developing new technology to create high-speed trains. One kind is based on electromagnets. These maglev trains can travel at speeds of around 300 miles an hour. That's a lot faster than the Tom Thumb!

What's It Called?

A locomotive is a railroad car that has an engine. A train is a line of connected railroad cars, pulled by an engine or locomotive. A railroad is system of transportation using trains.

MAKING A SOLAR-POWERED OVEN

You can make your very own solar-powered oven.
All you need to run it is the Sun.

You will need:

- pizza box
- black construction paper
- foil
- heavy clear plastic
- glue
- tape
- safety scissors
- ruler
- pencil
- plastic straw

1. Cut along three sides of the top of the pizza box, 1 inch from the edge. Do not cut the back edge.

2. Fold along the back edge to form a flap.

3. Glue foil smoothly onto the flap facing into the box.

foil

plastic

4. Cut a piece of plastic slightly larger than the flap opening. Tape it down over the opening.

5. Glue foil onto the inside bottom of the box. Tape black construction paper over this foil.

6. Close the top of the box. Prop the flap open with the straw.

7. Choose a food that just needs to be heated or melted, such as bread with cheese. Put your food inside the box. Place it outside so that the Sun shines on the foil.

8. See what happens!

straw

tortilla pizza ▶

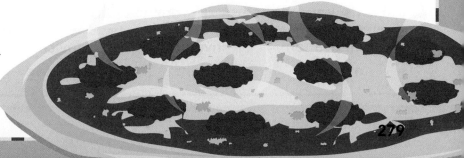

Retell "Margaret Knight: A Lifetime of Inventions!"

"Margaret Knight: A Lifetime of Inventions!" is a biography. It tells about the life of an inventor. Review the selection on pages 258–267. Look at the flow chart on page 281.

■ First Row of Pictures: What are some things Margaret Knight invented as a child?

■ Third Picture: What was her most important invention?

■ Fourth and Fifth Pictures: What did she have to do after her invention? What happened last of all?

Use the pictures on page 281 to retell the selection to your partner. As you talk about each idea or fact, point to the correct picture. Use complete sentences.

Words you might use in your retelling:

innovation	invention	device
model	patent	improve

toy inventions

safety idea

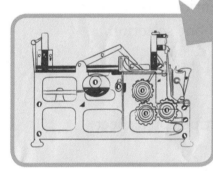

machine to
make bags

court

patent

Dig Deeper

Look Back

Work with a partner. Look through the unit and choose two inventions that have improved daily life. Answer the following questions about them.

1. What two inventions did you choose?

2. How did you and your partner narrow down your choices to two?

3. Which selections tell about the inventions you chose? (Some items are found in more than one selection.)

4. What specific problem does each solve to make life easier for people?

Each partner should answer these questions on a sheet of paper.

Talk About It

> Jung Ming got up before sunrise, and **he** worked on the railroad until long after dark. **He** dug holes, cleared rocks, shoveled dirt, cut down trees, and built bridges. Every night **his** back and arms ached, and **his** legs were sore.

In each sentence above, what person's name could substitute for *he* or *his*? Is it the same person's name in each sentence?

Work with a partner. Make up three sentences about someone you read about in the unit. Use *he, him,* or *his* or use *she* or *her* in each sentence. Have your partner see whether you used the words correctly.

Conversation

> Sometimes a friend asks you how to do something. Then you need to give clear instructions. Always give each step in order. Use words like *first, second, next,* and *finally.*

Talk to a partner. One of you will be person A. The other will be person B.

Person A   **Person B**

Tell the first step of
how to do something.

Ask what you need
to do next.

Tell the next step.

Guess the third step.
Tell your partner.

Give the correct
third step if your
partner was wrong.

Thank your
partner.

Earth, Moon, and Sun

The **BIG** Question

What can we learn from exploring the solar system?

☐ What milestones of space travel do you know about?

☐ What is it like to live on a space station?

☐ What do scientists and astronauts try to learn in space?

What have we discovered about our solar system?

1. What do we know about our planet?

Planet Earth...

☐ rotates on an axis.

☐ revolves around the Sun.

☐ has just one moon.

2. What can we see in outer space?

In outer space, we can see...

☐ our Sun.

☐ our Moon.

☐ stars.

☐ other planets in our solar system.

3. What are the other planets in our solar system like?

The other planets…

☐ revolve around the Sun, like Earth.

☐ probably have no plants or animals.

☐ are many different sizes.

☐ can have two moons, many moons, or no moons.

4. How have people learned about outer space?

People have…

☐ looked through telescopes.

☐ launched spacecraft.

☐ landed on the Moon.

☐ sent rovers to Mars.

Say **more!**

Theme Vocabulary

distance
inner planets
outer planets
astronomy
axis
rover
revolve
oxygen

The easiest way to remember the meaning of a new word is to use it. As you discuss the solar system, use these vocabulary words. Use them when you read and write about the solar system, too.

Read the word.
Look at the picture.
Use the word in a sentence.

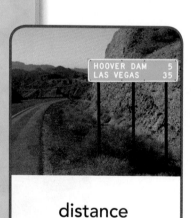

distance

inner planets

outer planets

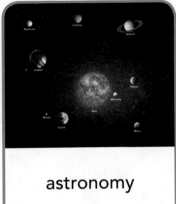

astronomy

axis

rover

revolve

oxygen

Which Picture?

Look at the vocabulary cards. Choose one picture. Don't tell anyone what it is! Describe the picture. See if your partner can guess which picture you chose.

King of the Game

1. WELCOME TO PLANET ZORK. WE SPEAK ZORK HERE. IF YOU CAN SPEAK ZORK, PRESS PLAY. NO ENGLISH BEYOND THIS POINT.

2. My name is José.
I am king of the Zork machine.
When it comes to speaking Zork,
I am supreme.

3. VROCK
BORT
GLURE

When I am on Zork,
I can say this and that.
I can speak Zork
at the drop of a hat.

4. One thing that hurts me,
I can't take anymore,
Is the name of the player
who has the top score.

DARK BART...6

...5

It's "Dark Bart" on top
with six million and nine,
while the other top scores
are mine, mine, mine, MINE.

5 I came in on Sunday.
   Deera came with me.
   She's a big pain,
   like shoes that don't fit me.

She doesn't speak Zork,
   but she just had to see
If I made a mistake
   when a Zork spoke to me.

6

7 I dropped in my coins
   and started to play,
I was thinking in Zork
   of what I should say.

HIG,
BOR,
MOAR,
DEM

..5,010,000

8 When I got a total for
   game number four,
I was far, far behind
   my top Zork game score.

9 I turned to Deera,
   "Little sis, honey,
Dig deep in your pocket
   and hand me some money."

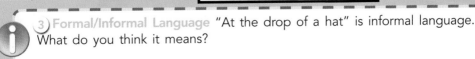

3 Formal/Informal Language "At the drop of a hat" is informal language. What do you think it means?

I went into a store
and asked for a meal.
I did it in Zork
that I knew was for real.

VO
GIB
SUM

11

She slid three more coins
into the slot.
When I heard them drop,
I knew I was hot.

10

I went to type JOSÉ
for the very best play,
But Deera jumped in
with D-E-E-R-A.

I got just what I asked for.
They rung it up then,
And I ended the game
with six million and ten.

12

13

10 **Expressions** "I knew I was hot" means "I knew I was good enough to win."

I said, "I am sorry
that you ever came."
She said, "No way, José.
My quarters, my game."

14

I went home thinking
that I did not care.
But I never got past it.
It just wasn't fair.

15

With six coins in hand,
I came back to Big Jake's.
I was all set to win
with whatever it takes.

16

DEERA...10,000,004

I was stunned for a moment
when I saw the top score.
It read DEERA
with ten million and four!

17

17 **Formal/Informal Language** José uses formal language when he says he "was stunned for a moment" when he sees Deera's score. How could he say this informally?

293

EVERYONE'S
EARTH, MOON, AND SUN
by Vladimir Rostov

Everyone is different. We are from different countries. We dress, eat, and play differently. We like different things. We wear different kinds of clothes, enjoy different books, and play different games.

But there is something that we all have in common. We all live on the same planet. We all live on Earth.

No matter where on Earth we are, when we look up at the sky, we all see the same Sun. When we look up at night, we all see the same Moon.

The Moon is the heavenly body closest to Earth. It is just under 239,000 miles from our planet.

The Sun is just under 93 million miles from Earth. That is 93,000,000 miles!

Sun ★ 太陽 ★ mặt trời ★ HNUB ★ Sol

Every language has its own names for Earth, the Moon, and the Sun.

Earth is one of the **inner planets**. The others are Mercury, Venus, and Mars. Those planets are closest to the Sun.

Earth **revolves** around the Sun. It takes Earth a year to complete its orbit all the way around the Sun.

Earth spins while it moves around the Sun. It takes 24 hours to rotate on its axis. An **axis** is an imaginary line around which a solid body turns.

Earth's rotation is what causes day and night. It is daytime in the places on Earth that face the Sun. It is nighttime in the places that face away from the Sun.

Awesome Planet

by Jill Jones

Captain Xing entered the starship's Situation Room. He chose a chair from the drop-down 3-D menu, waited for it to achieve material form, and took a seat. The others were already there.

"There's a problem, Captain," said Baade. "We can't possibly get near that planet. It's got a force field like you wouldn't believe."

The Captain flinched. "And what about its twin? Can we make it there?"

Wellstone shook his head. "Afraid not, Captain. The place is crawling with mutants."

It looked like the expedition to find a new planetary home was one big failure. They'd have to go back home and tell the people that there was no place else to go.

All of the sudden, a drop-down screen appeared. On it was a holographic message. The crew read it in silence. Then an image of a planet appeared.

"Wow," said Bissell. "Will you look at that! What an awesome planet! Do you think there's a chance . . . ?"

"Yes! Yes!" said Rodriguez excitedly. "The conditions are favorable! Plenty of sparkling lakes, majestic mountains, abundant forests, grassy fields! Everything anyone could ever want!"

"Unbelievable! It looks like a giant blue marble!" said Captain Xing. "Does it mention a name?"

"Yes. Here it is, at the bottom of the screen," said Rodriguez. "I believe the planet is called—Earth."

Men and Women in Space

by Gregory Rubin

We will never be able to fly to the Sun. It is much too hot to land on, and it is millions of miles away. That would be a very long **flight**!

The Moon is much closer to the Earth. If you look at the Moon through a **telescope**, it seems even closer. You can see the **craters** that cover its surface.

The Moon is even close enough to visit. That's just what astronaut Neil Armstrong did. In 1969, Armstrong and two other astronauts flew to the Moon in a **spacecraft** called *Apollo 11.*

The trip to the Moon took four days. The astronauts left the spacecraft and landed on the Moon's surface in a smaller craft called the *Eagle.* Then Armstrong stepped out of the *Eagle* and became the first person to walk on the Moon.

There is no **oxygen** on the Moon. Armstrong had to wear a spacesuit and carry special **equipment** so he could breathe.

Only twelve men have ever landed on the Moon. Some of them drove a **rover** on the Moon's surface. The last **lunar** landing was in 1972. People have not been back to the Moon since then. But many astronauts have flown in space.

It's not easy to become an astronaut. You must study and train. Why is it so challenging?

Astronauts must work under unusual conditions. Being an astronaut can be dangerous. One decision can mean the difference between life and death.

Astronauts must learn a lot about science, math, **astronomy**, and engineering. They must learn to operate different kinds of machinery and computer systems. They have to pass a physical exam to make sure they are healthy and fit.

Over five hundred men and women have gone into space. Many are from the United States and Russia. Russian men and women who fly in space are called *cosmonauts*, not *astronauts*. There are also astronauts from countries all over the globe, including China, India, and Poland.

In 1962, seven years before Armstrong's moonwalk, John Glenn became the first American to orbit the Earth. He flew all the way around our planet.

In 1983, Guy Bluford became the first African American to travel into space. As well as being a good astronaut, he wanted to be a role model for other young African Americans.

The same year, Sally Ride became the first American woman in space. As of now, over fifty women have flown in space.

Mae Jemison was the first African American woman to fly in space. She is also a physician. Today she works to make sure school kids learn about science and math so that they can become doctors, astronauts, and scientists, too.

Franklin Chang-Díaz is from Costa Rica and became a United States citizen. He has flown in space seven different times!

Russia, China, and many other countries have cooperated with one another to construct **space stations**. Koichi Yakata, a Japanese astronaut who is also an engineer, helped build one.

Thanks to space stations, astronauts can stay in space for weeks or even months at a time. One Russian cosmonaut stayed in a space station for over a year!

Over 200 astronauts from countries all over the world have visited a space station. A stay on a space station can be hard work. Astronauts may have to do repairs or conduct science experiments. For example, Susan Helms made repairs to a space station from outside the station. Ellen Ochoa did research on the Earth's climate and environment from space.

So did Edward Lu. His experiments helped us learn more about the sun. Today he is building a telescope to **launch** into space.

With the powerful telescopes we have here on Earth, we can see far beyond the **outer planets** at the edge of our solar system.

But with Lu's telescope, we will be able to see objects an even longer **distance** away. These objects are much too far away to see from telescopes here at home.

Prove It

What evidence does the author use to show that people from more than one country have traveled in space?

DAY AND

by Lynelle H. Morgenthaler

Cycles go round and round
Like a nonstop revolving door.
Just when you think you're done,
They come around for more!
On planet Earth, day turns to night,
And then night turns into day.
Twenty-four hours,
each day of the week,
It always happens that way.

NIGHT

Because Earth is spinning 'round
As it travels around the Sun,
Day is ending in China
When in New York, it's just begun.
    At any moment somewhere on Earth,
It is both day and night.
My morning may be your dinnertime
And my darkness may be your light!

MOON GAMES

by Andrew Miller

A play in two scenes

CAST OF CHARACTERS

FELIPE MAGAÑA,
a ten-year-old boy

MR. MAGAÑA, *Felipe's dad*

ASTROPILOT IRINA SEROVA

SPACE ALIEN #1

SPACE ALIEN #2

SCENE 1

After the audience is seated, the lights in the theater go out. It is as dark as outer space. Then the curtain goes up. There are no lights onstage. Then, suddenly, a spotlight comes on and shines on the Space Aliens, who are already standing onstage. They speak in funny voices and wear silly clothes.

SPACE ALIEN #1: The year: 2064. The planet: Earth.

SPACE ALIEN #2: The country: The United States of America. The city: Washington, DC.

SPACE ALIEN #1: The place: The home of Felipe Magaña.

(*The* SPACE ALIENS *exit. The stage lights go up. We are in the Magañas' kitchen.*)

MR. MAGAÑA: The food in these tubes is delicious. No wonder the astronauts love to eat it.

(FELIPE MAGAÑA *runs in, excited.*)

FELIPE: Papa! I won! I won the competition. I am one of the best athletes in the whole city of Washington, DC.

MR. MAGAÑA: That's wonderful, Felipe. (*He hugs* FELIPE.)

FELIPE: I was chosen to compete in the Moon Games next month.

MR. MAGAÑA: I wonder what your great-grandmother would think. She invented a way to add oxygen to the air on the Moon and on the inner planets. She loved to walk and drive a rover on the Moon.

FELIPE: Yes. You've told me the story. She liked to go to Mars, too. It used to take her many days to get to the Moon. Now that we can travel at 50,000 miles an hour, it will take me only a few hours.

MR. MAGAÑA: But it still takes weeks to get to Mars. That's much too long a trip for me.

FELIPE: I would still like to visit someday. Can we go if I do well at the Moon Games?

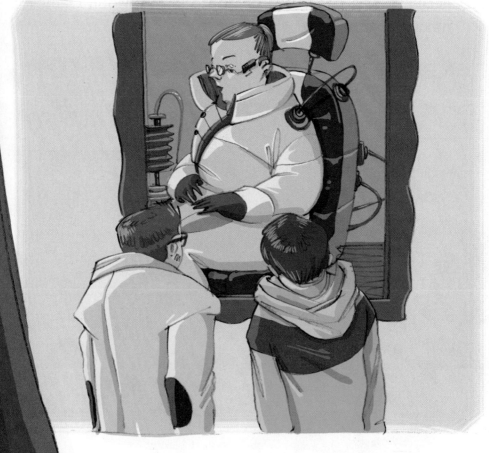

MR. MAGAÑA: Yes. That's a great idea. That will be a good incentive for you to work hard and do your best.

FELIPE: I'm going to practice and work out very hard for the next month. I'll be in great shape when I get to the Lunar Sports Village.

MR. MAGAÑA: OK. But you still have to do your schoolwork. I want you to do well in astronomy, robotics, space history, and English.

FELIPE: Oh, Dad. I already know about astronomy. I'd rather be learning about lunar flight science. Besides, I need time to work on my long-distance jumping.

MR. MAGAÑA: No complaining, Felipe.

FELIPE (*sighing*): OK, Dad. But I still want to spend every morning at the Anti-Gravity Stadium training with my teammates.

MR. MAGAÑA (*thinking*): Well, you should practice somewhere without gravity because there is so little gravity on the Moon. We'll talk about it. Right now it's dinnertime.

(**FELIPE** *sits down, and* **MR. MAGAÑA** *sets some tubes in front of him.*)

FELIPE: Ugh. This tastes like moon rocks. You're a wonderful dad, but you're a terrible cook.

SCENE 2

(*The* **SPACE ALIENS** *are standing onstage.*)

SPACE ALIEN #1: The time: One month later.

SPACE ALIEN #2: The place: Inside the Spaceship Armstrong.

> ### Zoom In
>
> Why does Felipe's father agree that it is a good idea to practice where there is little gravity?

SPACE ALIEN #1: It is on its way to the Moon.

SPACE ALIEN #2: We launched from the John Glenn Memorial Spaceport approximately two hours ago.

SPACE ALIEN #1: We will land at the Sally Ride Lunar Spaceport in approximately two hours.

SPACE ALIEN #2: The Moon Games begin in three days.

(*The* **SPACE ALIENS** *get into the rocket ship.* **FELIPE** *is already seated there.* **IRINA SEROVA** *is piloting the ship.*)

IRINA SEROVA: How are you doing back there, Felipe?

FELIPE: Much better now that you turned on the artificial gravity.

IRINA: Yes, it's difficult to travel so fast and float around the spacecraft at the same time. It took me a long time to get used to.

SPACE ALIEN #1: I prefer floating around to sitting down.

SPACE ALIEN #2: Me, too. But today we must make Felipe as comfortable as possible.

IRINA: He has to be ready to compete in three days.

SPACE ALIEN #1 (*to FELIPE*): Are you nervous?

FELIPE: I'm excited. I've trained and practiced all month. The coach and all my teammates say I'll do well.

SPACE ALIEN #2 (*pointing out the window*): A comet!

SPACE ALIEN #1: And you can see Mars in the distance!

FELIPE: From up here, you can really see that the Earth is a sphere, just like the globe in our classroom. It's beautiful. Look at the clouds swirling below. I can see the North American continent.

SPACE ALIEN #2: Can you see Washington, DC?

FELIPE: Of course not. We are much too far away.

IRINA: Why don't you look through this telescope?

FELIPE: Wow! I can see Washington, DC! I can even make out some of the monuments. I can see the outer planets, too.

SPACE ALIEN #2: Can you see Saturn? That's the planet with all the beautiful rings around it.

SPACE ALIEN #1: And look for Jupiter. Earth has only one moon, but Jupiter has over 60!

FELIPE: I can't wait to get to Earth's moon and the Moon Games!

> ### Zoom In
>
> What does Felipe see out of the window of the spaceship?

SPACE ALIEN #2: What events are you competing in?

FELIPE: I'm going to be in weightlifting, the long jump, and the high jump.

SPACE ALIEN #1: You'll do well. There's not much gravity on the Moon, so you can lift six times as much weight as you can on Earth and jump six times as high.

IRINA: That's true. But so can everyone else!

FELIPE: Boys and girls from all over the solar system will be there. I'm mostly worried about one girl who grew up in the Earth colony on Mars. She can jump higher than any other Martian.

IRINA: Look, everyone. We're almost there.

FELIPE: Up close, the Moon looks so different. It's covered with craters. There are mountains, too. The surface is all sandy and rocky. There are no plants or trees.

IRINA: Nope. There's no water, either. The surface is like a desert.

IRINA: Prepare for touchdown! Hang on, everyone!

FELIPE: We're on the Moon! There's the Lunar Sports Village.

(*The* SPACE ALIENS *and* FELIPE *exit the spacecraft.*)

IRINA, SPACE ALIEN #1 AND #2: Good luck, Felipe!

Prove It

What is different about the setting of Scene 1 and that of Scene 2? Where did you find your evidence?

LIFE ABOARD A SPACE STATION

by Carmela Ramirez

Gravity is an invisible force. Although we can't see it, it affects everything we do.

Gravity pulls everything toward the Earth. If you drop an egg, it falls down and cracks. Everything on Earth falls to the ground unless there is something holding it up. That's because of gravity.

But there is very little gravity on a space station. There is no force to hold things down. If you let go of an egg in space, it does not fall down. It floats around instead.

The lack of gravity makes it difficult to do even ordinary things. Scientists must invent special ways to do just about everything. It takes a lot of practice.

Living in space is different in other ways, too. There is no oxygen in space, and it is very cold. So astronauts need special equipment to breathe and stay warm.

Astronauts must bring everything they will eat and drink with them. If they remain in space for a long time, that's a lot of food. It's like going on a very long camping trip.

Astronauts must plan very carefully. If they forget something, they can't go back and get it!

Eating

Space stations are supplied with many different kinds of foods and drinks. Astronauts eat fruits, nuts, peanut butter, chicken, beef, seafood, and brownies. They can drink coffee, tea, orange juice, and lemonade. There are no refrigerators on a space station. The food must be specially packaged so that it doesn't spoil. The space station does have an oven so the astronauts can heat up their food.

Because there is very little gravity, astronauts use straps to hold down their food trays. Magnets keep their forks, spoons, and knives on the trays. They drink through straws.

Sleeping

We sleep in beds under the covers. Astronauts sleep in sleeping bags they attach to a wall so they don't float around.

The men and women on a space station sleep for eight hours. But they do not use alarm clocks. The people in charge of the space flight, who are here on Earth, wake them up with music every morning.

Washing

When you turn on a shower here on Earth, the water flows down. If you take a bath, the water stays in the tub. In space, the water would go all over the place.

It is important for astronauts to stay clean in space so they don't spread germs. They wash with wet, soapy cloths or sponges. Instead of using a towel to dry off, they use a small vacuum cleaner! That keeps all the water in one place.

They use a toothbrush, toothpaste, dental floss, combs, and razors just as they would on Earth.

Dressing

Astronauts wear special spacesuits when they are launching and landing their spacecrafts. But the astronauts aboard the space station wear regular clothes.

They bring as little with them as possible to save room. But there are no washing machines. They must save water for more important things, anyway. So they only change their clothes every ten days. But they change their underwear and socks every other day.

Their clothes have a lot of pockets to hold equipment. The pockets all have zippers to keep everything from floating out.

Working

Flying a spacecraft safely is a full-time job. But astronauts have other jobs, too.

Some astronauts conduct science experiments in space. They want to learn how plants grow and how tools work in an environment with very little gravity.

Others learn about how their own bodies function in a weightless environment. Still others explore space through telescopes. From space, they can see things that we can't see from Earth.

Exercising

To become an astronaut, you have to be in tip-top physical shape. Astronauts must also stay in good shape while they are in space. They are required to exercise for two hours a day.

On a space station, there is an exercise bicycle that astronauts can ride. They also use a treadmill. A treadmill is a piece of equipment that you can run and walk on.

Zoom In

What details show that keeping clean in space is harder than keeping clean on Earth?

Relaxing

Even astronauts need to relax and have fun. Astronauts aboard a space station get weekends off. What do they do for fun?

The astronauts enjoy bouncing around inside the space station. They also watch movies, play video games, and read books. They can even play basketball!

The sights in space are unusual. Because a space station is so high above the Earth, astronauts can watch the sun rise and set every forty-five minutes. After they come home, they often talk about how beautiful it is in space.

What if they get homesick? Astronauts can communicate with their friends and families back on Earth.

Snacking in Space

If you eat a cookie at home, the crumbs get on the table or on the floor. But on a space station, they just float around in the air. They can get into the equipment and cause trouble. So the astronauts must be very careful when they have their snacks.

EARTH VS. SPACE

It only takes about three days to fly to the International Space Station. But once an astronaut gets there, things are very different from home.

	Earth	Space
Environment	Gravity	No gravity
Eating	Table	Magnetized trays and utensils
Food	Fresh	Specially packaged
Sleeping	Bed	Sleeping bag
Washing	Shower and towels	Wet cloths and vacuums
Dressing	Regular clothes	Clothes with lots of zippers
Exercising	Inside or outside	Stationary bike and treadmill
Working	Jobs such as office work	Flying a spacecraft, doing experiments
Relaxing	Any kind of fun	Views from space
Snacking	Any snacks	No crumbs!

Prove It

How are the rows in the chart related to the sections in the text?

Learn the Words

crater
spacecraft
equipment
flight
space station
launch
lunar
telescope

- Read the words on the list.
- Read the dialogue.
- Find the words.

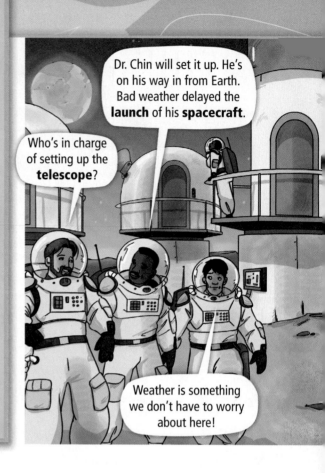

1. Write an Ad
Writing

Write an ad inviting people to a new lunar city, like the one in the picture. Tell why it would be exciting. Describe some of the things that have been built in the city. Tell how people would travel to the Moon. Show your ad to a partner. See if the ad can be improved.

2. Dialogue
Listening and Speaking

Work with your partner. You have just landed on the Moon. Your partner is there to greet you. Ask five questions about life on the Moon. Then, it's your partner's turn. Your partner should ask five questions about why you came and what your trip was like.

3. Take a Survey
Graphic Organizer

Ask at least five classmates where they want to travel in space. Tally their choices. Share your findings with your partner.

Where in Space Would You Travel?			
Moon	Mars	A Space Station	Another Planet

4. You Are the Reporter
Listening and Speaking

You are reporting on the launch of a spacecraft. Before you start, ask your partner about any vocabulary words you don't understand. Use at least three vocabulary words in your news story. Tell what happens. Quote some people who watch the launch. Tell how they feel about it. Read your report to the class.

Hanging Around in Space

by Courtney Hernandez

In the spring of 2002, two skillful astronauts took a spacewalk to improve safety on the International Space Station. The astronauts were American Franklin Chang-Díaz and his French crewmate, Phillippe Pérrin. It was the first time either of them had ever worked outside in space. On their other trips to the space station, they always stayed inside.

To make sure they didn't float away, they attached themselves to the station with very strong cables. Then they went outside to accomplish their tasks.

The two astronauts installed a robotic arm to make repairs outside the space station. The arm can be controlled from inside the space station. By staying inside, the astronauts can make these repairs more safely.

Chang-Díaz and Perrin also attached metal shields to the sides of the space station to make it safer. The shields protect the crew's living area from harmful objects that sometimes crash into the space station. This equipment is important to the safety of the astronauts.

The astronauts also inspected some broken equipment on the outside of the space station. They took photos and sent them back to scientists on Earth. The scientists were able to see the broken equipment and work with engineers to figure out a way to fix it.

The astronauts worked outside in space for more than seven hours. Later, they had to take two more spacewalks to fix other things. They spent 19 hours and 31 minutes in space.

The International Space Station is called "international" because astronauts from nations all over the world go there to work. Men and women from different countries fly there and work there together.

The International Space Station is an example of how different countries can cooperate with each other. They work together to learn more about science and space.

Prove It

What evidence shows why the space station is called the International Space Station?

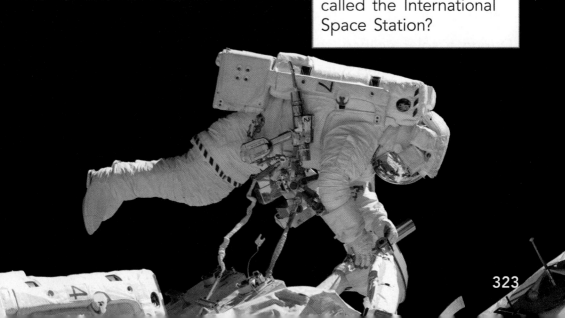

VISIT OUTER SPACE ON EARTH!

Take a trip to the Star Planetarium

It's like a museum about outer space! The mission of the Star Planetarium is to educate the public about the wonders of our universe in a comfortable, fun environment.

PERMANENT EXHIBIT: The Solar System Room

Walk among our models of the inner planets and the outer planets. Watch them revolve around the Sun while they rotate on their axis. See Earth the way astronauts see it from space—as a beautiful blue globe.

FEATURE: SPACE NEWS

Learn all about upcoming solar and lunar eclipses!

During a solar eclipse, the Moon comes between the Sun and Earth, and blocks out the Sun. It gets dark in the middle of the day. During a lunar eclipse, Earth's shadow blocks out the Moon at night.

Check here for the time of the next solar eclipse
Check here for the time of the next lunar eclipse

WELCOME TO THE STAR PLANETARIUM

▶ PLAN YOUR VISIT

Hours:
Weekdays: 9 A.M. to 6 P.M.
Tuesdays: until 9 P.M.
Weekends: 9 A.M. to 7 P.M.
Telescope open weekends until midnight

Admission:
$15 adults $10 members $5 students $25 family pass
Tuesdays after 6 P.M. are free!

▶ BECOME A MEMBER

Our members can come to the museum as often as they like for free. They can bring another person along as their guest. Membership costs $100 per year.

▶ CURRENT EXHIBITS

"Flying in Space" Take your seat on our space shuttle and find out what it's like to be an astronaut.

"Who Else Lives in Our Galaxy?" Could there be life on other planets? Find out.

"Go to the Moon" Put on a spacesuit and learn how it feels to walk on the Moon. Watch out for craters!

Retell "Moon Games"

 When you retell a story, you tell only the most important events. When you tell a story that is in the form of a play, you can often give the important events from each scene.

"Moon Games" is science fiction. It is set about fifty years in the future. Review the selection on pages 304–313. Look at the pictures on page 327.

■ Scene 1: What characters are in this scene? What has happened? What are the characters looking forward to?

■ Scene 2: What characters are in this scene? What happens during the scene? Where are the characters at the end?

Use the pictures on page 327 to retell the story to your partner. As you retell each part, point to the correct picture. Use complete sentences.

Words you might use in your retelling:		
distance	spacecraft	launch
flight	lunar	crater

Scene 1

Scene 2

Dig Deeper

Look Back

Look back at "Moon Games." Answer these questions on a sheet of paper.

1. What features tell you that this selection is a play?

2. Who would you say is the main character? What evidence did you use?

3. If "Moon Games" had one more scene at the end, what might it show? Tell what clues you used from the play.

4. What new characters might be in that new scene?

Talk About It

What would be good questions to ask an astronaut? Work with a partner.

Use what you have read in this unit.

Come up with four questions.

They do not have to be questions that are already answered in the selections.

If they are questions that have been answered, tell what answers the astronaut would probably give.

Conversation

> When people negotiate, they try to find a solution. They listen to each other. They try to learn what each person wants. They try to reach an agreement that helps both people.

Talk to a partner. One of you will be person A.
The other will be person B.

Person A

Suggest how you and your partner can work together on a project.

Reply. Tell why your solution is better.

Suggest a compromise.

Person B

Disagree. Suggest another way to share the work.

Reply. Tell why your solution is better.

Agree.
Tell what you both agree to do.

Pulse of LIFE

The **BIG** Question

What characteristics do all living things share?

☐ What do people need to do to keep their bodies healthy?

☐ How do the body's systems work together?

☐ What does each part of a plant do to help the plant live and grow?

Let's Talk

How are living things alike, and how are they different?

1. What are some characteristics of the human body?

The human body has…

☐ bones.

☐ muscles.

☐ nerves.

☐ organs.

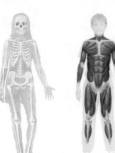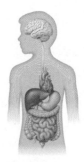

2. What are some characteristics of green plants?

Green plants…

☐ have chlorophyll in their leaves.

☐ can make their own food.

☐ get water from the ground through their roots.

☐ make oxygen for us to breathe.

3. What are some ways to stay healthy?

We can keep healthy by…

☐ eating right.

☐ getting enough exercise.

☐ getting checkups at the dentist.

☐ getting enough sleep.

4. How does exercise help us?

Exercise can…

☐ make our muscles stronger.

☐ help our heart pump better.

☐ help our lungs.

☐ help us fight sickness.

Say **more!**

coordinate
emotion
voluntary
involuntary
respiration
photosynthesis
chlorophyll
nutrients

Theme Vocabulary

The easiest way to remember the meaning of a new word is to use it. As you discuss how living things are alike and different, use these vocabulary words. Use them when you read and write about living things, too.

Read the word.
Look at the picture.
Use the word in a sentence.

coordinate

emotion

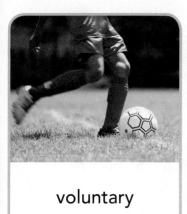

voluntary

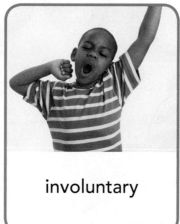

involuntary

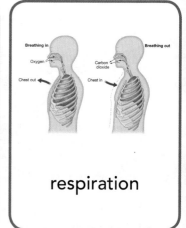

respiration

photosynthesis

chlorophyll

nutrients

How Do You Feel?

Look at the vocabulary cards. Choose one picture and tell how it makes you feel.

A Big Pain

Jay

Ray

1 This is my brother Jay. He's a big pain in the neck. He gets me in hot water because he blames me for everything.

Who let the cat sit on my bed?

2

It's raining cats and dogs.

Who let the rain in to soak the rug?

3

It's the same old story every time.

Jay did it!

Ray did it!

4

1) **Formal/Informal Language** Calling someone "a big pain in the neck" is an informal way to say that the person is very annoying. Would you use this expression when speaking with an adult you don't know well?

A week later…

Who put a boat in the tub?

12

Who left the soap on the rug?

13

Jay is back to his old self again. Jay is a pain in the neck!

Ray did it!

14

14 **Expressions** Saying that someone "is back to his old self again" means that he "is behaving the way he usually does."

RECIPE FOR A HEALTHY BODY

[SERVES 1]

INGREDIENTS

8 HOURS OF SLEEP

3 HEALTHY MEALS

FLUIDS SUCH AS WATER
AND MILK

30 MINUTES OR MORE
OF EXERCISE

DASH OF HEALTHY SNACKS

1. Begin with 8 hours of sleep.
2. Add in 3 meals, beginning with breakfast.
3. Mix with enough **fluids**, such as plain water or milk.
4. Add in at least 30 minutes of the exercise of your choice, such as bike riding, jumping rope, baseball, basketball, or soccer.
5. Season with a dash of snacks.
6. Combine all ingredients thoroughly.
7. Use daily and enjoy.

Yields one healthy, happy body.

Remember to follow up with regular checkups with the doctor and dentist.

If you are sleepy, you won't be able to learn as well. You also won't have as much fun! If you are hungry, it can be hard to concentrate. Eat a good breakfast so you have the energy to enjoy your busy day.

Are you hungry again? Time for lunch! Just remember that your body needs foods that give you energy. Fast food and snack foods with lots of salt, sugar, and fat don't help you build your body. Neither does sugary soda.

Luckily, a lot of tasty foods are good for you, too. Meat, fish, chicken, beans, nuts, dairy products, and eggs should be on your menu. Also enjoy whole-grain foods, such as oatmeal, whole-grain bread and tortillas, and lots of fresh fruits and vegetables.

Exercise keeps your heart, muscles, and bones healthy. It makes you feel better and gives you more energy. It even helps you sleep better. And, of course, it's fun!

Poem

Growth Chart

by James Jackson

When I was little, just starting to walk

My mother took a piece of chalk.

She made a line upon the wall

and told me I was three feet tall.

She said that she would measure me

on every birthday just to see

how tall I'd gotten since the last time.

That became our favorite pastime!

And every year from then on in,

she'd take my measurements again.

I'd stand against the smudgy wall,

and hold my breath so I'd be tall.

Today's the day that I am ten.

It's time to measure me again!

I think it will be fun to see

Where on the wall the line will be!

Human Body Systems

by Sophia Nazari

Your body has many different systems. Each system has special jobs and is made up of many parts. All the systems **coordinate**, or work together, to do everything your body needs.

muscular system

When you think of muscles, you think of movement and strength. But helping you move around and lift things are just two of the jobs your muscles do. You have about 700 muscles in your body! Some muscles help you chew, swallow, and speak. Muscles around your eyes help you blink. There's even a muscle inside each of your eyes. This muscle helps your eyes adjust to see both close up and far away. Another kind of muscle helps you digest food. Your heart is also made of muscle.

Muscles are made up mostly of protein. This is why you need to eat protein every day. It helps build and repair your muscles. Fish, meat, soybeans, and eggs are examples of high-protein foods.

More facial muscles are used to frown than to smile.

nervous system

Your nervous system is made up of your brain, your spinal cord, and millions of **nerve** cells. Your brain is the control center of the nervous system. In fact, it's the control center of your entire body. The brain is the power behind almost everything you do, including moving, thinking, keeping your balance, and expressing **emotions**. There's even a part of the brain that regulates your breathing and your heartbeat! A **network** of nerves carries messages to and from your brain.

Your brain works whether you are awake or asleep. It does need rest, though. Getting enough rest helps your brain stay sharp so you can think fast and remember what you learn. Your brain also needs lots of energy in order to do its work. It gets energy from carbohydrates. Foods rich in healthful carbohydrates include whole grains, fruits, and vegetables.

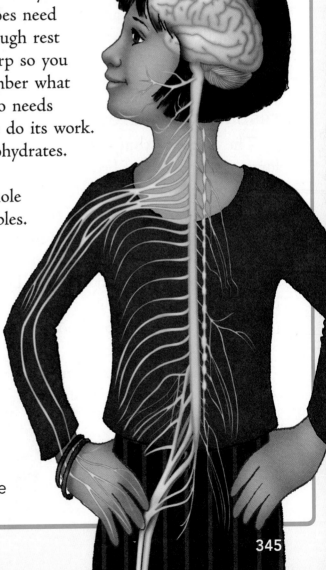

People do not stop thinking when they are asleep. Wow!

skeletal system

Your skeletal system includes all your bones. Your bones support your body and give it strength. You couldn't stand up or move without them! Another important job that bones do is to protect your body's organs, such as your brain, your heart, and your lungs.

Bones are made up largely of a mineral called calcium. This is why it's important to eat foods rich in calcium, such as milk, cheese, and leafy vegetables. Calcium helps your bones stay strong.

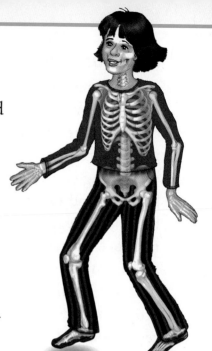

respiratory system

The center of your respiratory system is your lungs. The process of breathing is also called **respiration**. Your lungs get oxygen from the air. When you breathe in air through your nose and mouth, the air travels to your lungs. Your blood picks up oxygen from your lungs and carries it to your heart. That oxygen-rich blood is then pumped through your body. All of your cells need oxygen.

Your lungs work best when you get enough exercise. Don't just sit around playing computer games! Get up and run around, and your lungs will thank you.

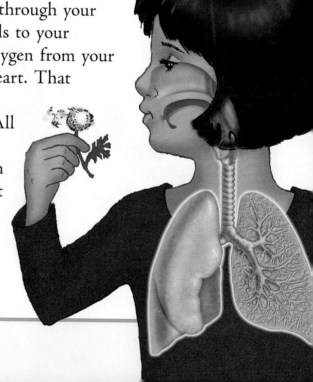

circulatory system

At the center of your circulatory system is your heart. Your heart acts like a pump. As it **contracts**, it pushes blood out through your body. The blood carries food and oxygen to every cell. After feeding your cells, blood returns to your heart. Your heart sends the blood to your lungs to get more oxygen. The oxygen-rich blood returns to your heart and is pumped back out to feed your cells again.

Blood cells are made largely of iron. You can help your blood by eating foods rich in iron, such as meat, eggs, seafood, and some kinds of beans.

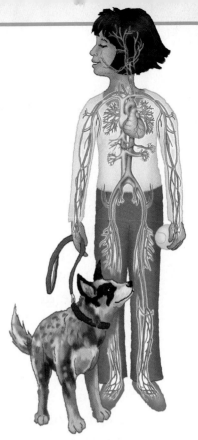

digestive system

Your digestive system handles everything you eat and drink. It breaks down the food and fluids into elements that your body can use. These elements include vitamins, minerals, protein, fats, and carbohydrates. The food you digest helps all the other systems in your body to work.

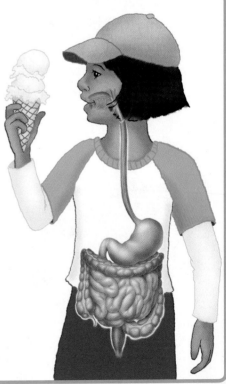

Prove It

How do the headings help you read and understand the article?

347

Monsoon and Me

by Quan Cao

Drop by drop,
all around me,
right over me,
on my tongue,
tasting like dew,
soaking me,
becoming me.

Tickling my throat,
it descends into
the center of my being.
It becomes me,
and the blood rushes
through my veins,
nourishing my world,
one with Mother Nature
once again.

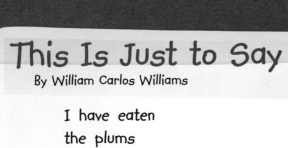

This Is Just to Say

By William Carlos Williams

I have eaten
the plums
that were in
the icebox

and which
you were probably
saving
for breakfast

Forgive me
they were delicious
so sweet
and so cold.

Plants Are Alive!

by Susan Guthrie

What makes a plant a plant? Can you tell just by looking? A daffodil is a plant, but so is a giant redwood tree. So is a cactus covered with sharp spines, and so is a blade of grass.

There are hundreds of thousands of different plants, but almost all of them share a few important **characteristics**. Take a closer look at the plants around you. Why are so many of them green? Why do they need stems? What is the purpose of their roots? Let's look at the parts of a plant and do some experiments to see how they work.

What Are the Parts of a Flowering Plant?

flower

stem

leaves

roots

Green plants like this flower are alive. They grow. If they are flowering plants, flowers bud and bloom. Some plants produce new leaves every spring. Most plants produce seeds that will make new plants. To do all these tasks, plants need water, **nutrients**, soil, and sunlight. All the plant parts work together to help the plant get what it needs.

How Does a Plant Get Water?

Plants need water to grow, but they can't just grab it out of the air. Do this experiment to learn how plants get water.

1. Place two plants in a sunny spot.

2. Cut a cup as shown below.

3. Wrap one plant with the cup, covering the soil.

4. Water just the leaves of the covered plant.

5. Water the soil of the other.

6. Observe them after one week.

After a week, the leaves on the covered plant may have become wilted and dry. Pouring water on leaves can clean off their surface, but it doesn't provide food. That's why plants depend on their roots. The second plant is nice and healthy because water was poured directly onto the soil, which contains nutrients. The water picked up those nutrients and carried them along to the roots. The plant's roots absorbed the water and nutrients.

Roots take in water. ▲

How Does a Plant Get Food?

Plants need more than the nutrients in the soil, but you don't have to feed them. They make their own food. This experiment will show you the parts of a plant that make food.

1. Start with two matching plants.

2. Place one in a dark closet. Put the other by a sunny window.

3. Water both plants.

4. Check on the plants after two weeks.

The plant from the closet may now have pale patches on its leaves. The leaves may also look droopy or wilted. What did the healthy plant have that the other one didn't? Sunlight! Plants make food by changing the light energy from the Sun into food. This process is called **photosynthesis**. For this process, plants need **chlorophyll**, which they make and store in their leaves. Chlorophyll is what makes plants green.

When photosynthesis occurs, oxygen is released into the air. Humans and animals need oxygen for respiration. It can truly be said that without green plants, there would be no people or land animals on this planet.

Zoom In

Why did the plant in the closet look droopy? Where did you find your answer?

How Does a Plant Get Nutrients to All Its Parts?

Plants have a system for delivering nutrients to all of their parts. You'll see how it's done in this experiment.

step 1

1. Fill a glass with water.

step 2

2. Add ten drops of blue food coloring.

step 3

3. Cut off the end of the stem of a white flower.

step 4

4. Put the flower in the water. Observe the flower for four days.

Zoom In

What are the main steps in the experiment on this page?

The flower may now be blue. You can see how water and nutrients are carried to the flower through the stem. The fluid travels through tiny tubes inside the stem.

This process is the same whether the plant is a single rose on a stem or a large bush full of berries or even a 200-year-old oak tree. A tree's trunk is really a giant, woody stem.

▲ Blue food coloring inside the stem

How Do Different Plant Parts Help a Plant?

Your experiments have shown how the different parts of a plant work and how each part contributes to the plant's overall health.

1. Roots keep a plant in place and help it take in fluids from the soil.

2. The stem carries water and nutrients up from the roots.

3. Leaves use sunlight to make the plant's food.

2. stem

3. leaves

1. roots

Prove It

How did the diagrams help you understand the information in this selection?

Plants come in many sizes and shapes. They grow in the frozen Arctic; in the hot, dry deserts of Africa; in the moist rain forests of South America; and in the highest mountains of Asia. Plants provide the raw materials for paper, musical instruments, clothing, dyes, and many medicines. They supply a huge variety of fruits, vegetables, herbs, and grains that are eaten by both people and animals. Through photosynthesis, they release oxygen into the air we breathe. Plants are alive, and your experiments have revealed some of the secrets about how they work.

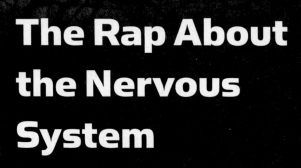

The Rap About the Nervous System

by Lynelle H. Morgenthaler
and Karen Clevidence

You've got nerve!
And so do I.
The nervous system's job is tough—
I'll tell you why!

There's a lot going on!
How **complex** could it be?
There's a brain, a spinal cord,
And lots of nerve cells in me.

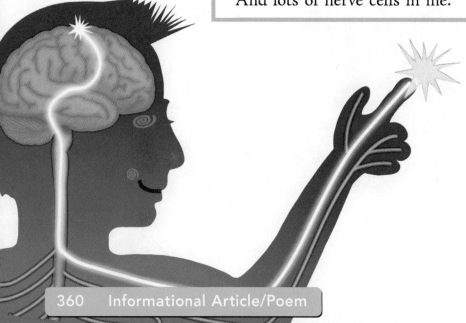

The nervous system controls what goes on inside your body. The parts of this system send messages back and forth day and night, all through your body. Your nervous system has many parts:

The Brain and Spinal Cord

+ The brain is the manager, or "boss," of the entire nervous system. Every signal or message must go through the brain.

+ Your spinal cord stretches from your brain down your back. It is like the main cable in an electrical grid.

Nerves and Nerve Endings

+ Nerves are bundles of special fibers. Nerves branch out from the spinal cord and stretch throughout the body.

+ Nerves are like messengers. They form networks to carry messages from the brain and spinal cord to every part of your body. They also carry information back to the central nervous system.

What Nerves Do

Nerves help you:

+ move everything from your arms, legs, fingers, and toes to your eyelids and lips.

+ feel sensations (hot, cold, pain, itching).

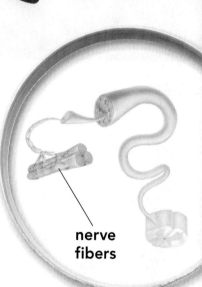

nerve fibers

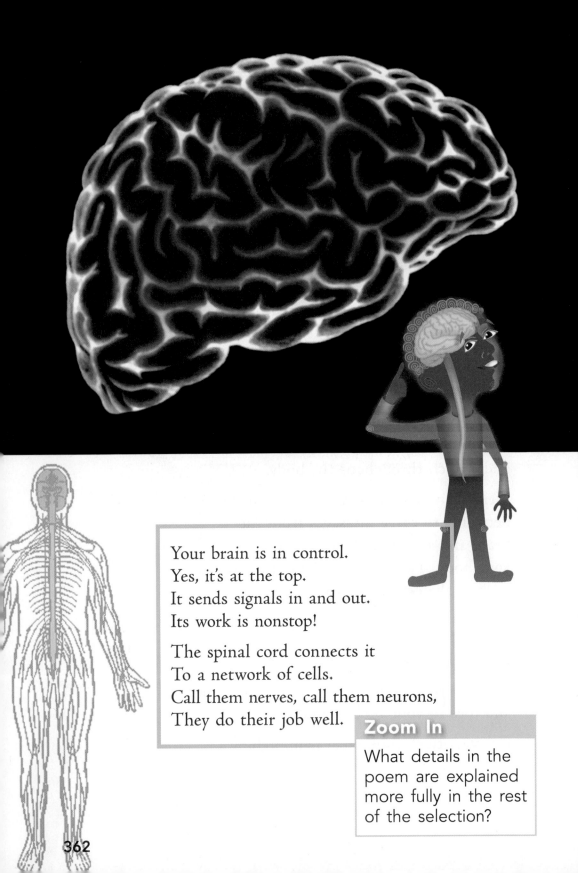

Your brain is in control.
Yes, it's at the top.
It sends signals in and out.
Its work is nonstop!

The spinal cord connects it
To a network of cells.
Call them nerves, call them neurons,
They do their job well.

Zoom In

What details in the
poem are explained
more fully in the rest
of the selection?

The Brain Has Three Main Parts

1. The Cerebrum

The cerebrum controls thinking and **voluntary** movements, such as turning a page in this book. It is by far the largest section of the brain. It is more complex than the most advanced computer. It can do more things than any computer, and it can do many things at the same time. The cerebrum can help you:

+ plan for the future.

+ remember the past.

+ make judgments.

+ solve math problems.

+ make up a song.

2. The Cerebellum

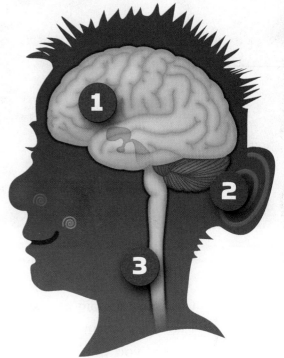

The cerebellum coordinates movements and helps you keep your balance. It also lets you know where your body is in relation to other things. This allows you to:

+ climb stairs, because you know how high to lift your foot.

+ eat with a fork or spoon, because you know where to bring your hand to reach your mouth.

3. The Brain Stem

The brain stem connects the brain to the spinal cord. It controls **involuntary** actions. These are actions you don't think about. Your body's involuntary actions include digesting food, breathing regularly, and your heartbeat.

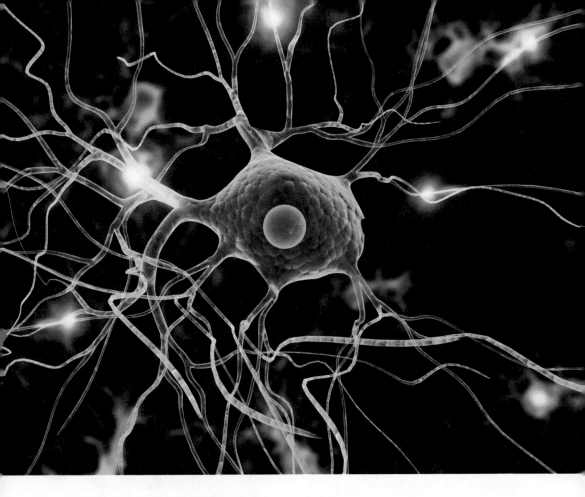

Their game is delivery
Of messages big and small.
Like a guy bringing pizza,
Except you don't see them at all!

So when you use a sense,
Like taste or feel or touch,
A message goes to your brain
So you can say, "Yuck!"

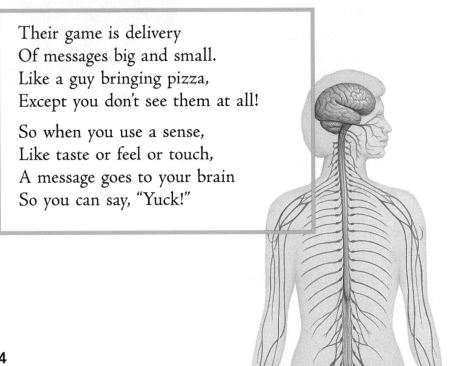

- **Sensory Receptors** gather information from inside your body.

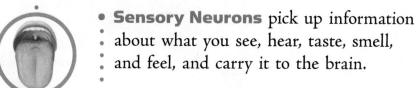

- **Sensory Neurons** pick up information about what you see, hear, taste, smell, and feel, and carry it to the brain.

- **The Brain** decides what to do and sends back a message.

- **Motor Neurons** carry the brain's message telling the body what action to take.

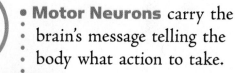

Messages carried by the sensory and motor neurons happen very quickly.

Prove It

How do the pictures in this selection help you to understand the text?

Learn the Words

characteristic
network
nerves
pulse
complex
contract
rate
fluid

- Read the words on the list.
- Read the dialogue.
- Find the words.

I've checked your **pulse rate**, and it's normal.

I can stretch and **contract** this muscle without pain. I know I'll run well today!

Isn't water wonderful? It's the best **fluid** to drink during a run.

As ice, it helps sore muscles.

1. You Are the Actor
Listening and Speaking

Work with a partner. Ask your partner about any vocabulary words you don't understand. Then take turns reading the dialogue in the picture above. Use your best acting voice. Make the dialogue come alive.

2. You Are the Author
Writing

Soda and other sugary drinks are not good for you. However, it is important to drink fluids every day. Think of at least three healthful fluids to drink. Write a paragraph. Tell which fluids you think are the best to drink every day.

3. Talk About Devices
Listening and Speaking

Some devices are simple. A pencil is an example. It is easy to use. Other devices are complex. Work with a partner. Think of five simple devices and five complex devices. Tell the class about them. Explain what makes them simple or complex.

4. Make a Venn Diagram
Graphic Organizer

Work with a partner. Think of two different kinds of animals. Think of four characteristics of each animal. Fill in the Venn diagram. In the middle oval, put characteristics that both animals share.

Traits of Two Animals

[animal] both [animal]

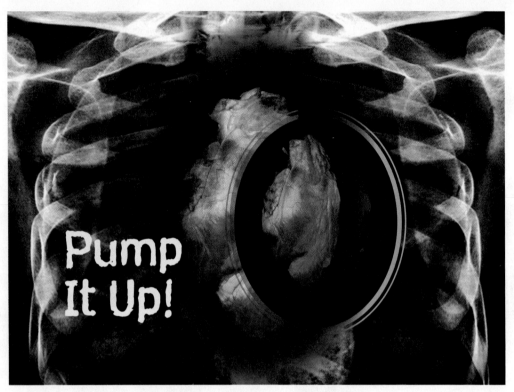

Pump It Up!

by Sarita Chávez Silverman

In a way, your heart is just like the rest of the muscles in your body. It contracts to do its job. Then it relaxes. When the heart muscle contracts, it pumps blood through a complex network of blood vessels all over your body. When it relaxes, blood flows back into the heart.

Your heart is different from other muscles in some ways, however. For one thing, it is made of special muscle fibers that are not found in any of your other muscles. Heart muscle fibers are adapted not to get tired. After all, your heart must keep doing its job 24 hours a day, even when you are asleep.

Another difference is that most of the other muscles in your body are voluntary. You have to think about making them work. If you draw a circle, you must cause your hand to hold the pencil and make the shape.

But the heart muscle is involuntary. It works all on its own. You don't have to think about making your heart beat.

Have you ever felt your heart thumping in your chest? Certain emotions, such as fear, anger, or excitement, increase the number of times your heart beats per minute. You can't control how these emotions change your heart **rate.**

However, there are things you can do on purpose to make your heart pump faster. When you exercise, all the muscles in your body need more blood. So your heart works harder and faster to pump all that blood around your body.

Like your other muscles, your heart needs exercise. To improve your heart's health, you must get the kind of exercise that raises your heart rate for at least thirty minutes.

You can run, swim, dance, or even just walk at a good pace. You already play lots of sports that are good for your heart, such as basketball and soccer.

However, some things we do for fun do not improve our heart's health. Sitting at the computer does not work your muscles, so it doesn't raise your heart rate.

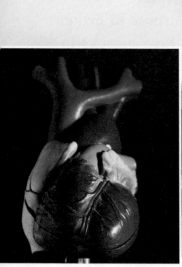

Your **pulse** is a measurement of how many times per minute your heart beats. Place two fingers on the inside of your wrist, or on your neck just below your ear. That's where there are large blood vessels very close to the skin's surface. You will be able to feel your own pulse. You can feel your heart pumping blood through your body!

Your pulse rate goes up when your heart beats faster. One way to raise your pulse rate is to run or jump for a few minutes. Being under stress or having a fever will also raise your heart rate.

If your muscles are strong, they will be able to do more work more easily. Your leg muscles are designed to help you run. The stronger your leg muscles, the less tired you get when you run.

Your heart works the same way. The stronger it is, the more easily it can do what it is meant to do. A strong heart does not have to work as hard to pump blood around your body. So a strong heart does not need to beat as frequently.

Believe it or not, athletes' hearts beat more slowly than the hearts of people who sit around. Athletes' pulse rates do not increase that much when they exercise. An athlete's resting pulse rate can be as low as 40 beats per minute.

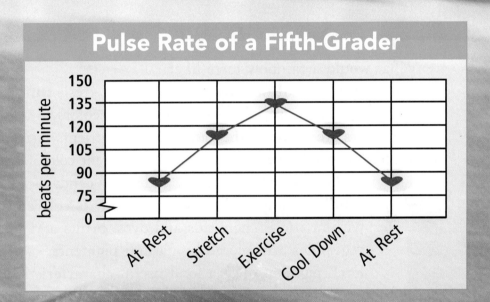

Pulse Rate of a Fifth-Grader

Prove It

How many beats per minute does the heart beat when a fifth-grader is exercising?

Eating the Rainbow

by Drew Gonzales

What would a rainbow taste like?

You can't eat a real rainbow, of course. But fresh fruits and vegetables come in a delicious rainbow of colors.

The colors are a clue to the vitamins and nutrients inside. That's because each nutrient turns food a different color.

Gumdrops, jellybeans, and other candy come in many colors, too. But candy is colored with artificial chemicals and dyes. Fruits and vegetables are colored by natural pigments. Each pigment gives a food useful characteristics.

Yellow and orange fruits and vegetables are high in vitamin A, which is important for your eyesight. Carrots, squash, sweet potatoes, mangos, peaches, papayas, and nectarines are all good sources of vitamin A.

Blue and purple pigment is found in eggplant, blueberries, and purple cabbage. These foods are good for your memory and your blood pressure.

White vegetables may help heart health. They include leeks, cauliflower, jicama, and parsnips. Some fruits and vegetables are a different color on the outside but white inside. They include turnips, bananas, and pears.

Green vegetables protect your vision. They also contain fiber, which keeps your digestive system healthy. Choose from collard greens, kale, broccoli, Brussels sprouts, celery, peas, spinach, and zucchini.

Red pigments contain nutrients that are good for your heart. You can find them in beets, red peppers, radishes, and tomatoes.

A balanced diet includes lots of fruits and vegetables. Eat them in all the colors of the rainbow, and you will never grow tired of them. Each one tastes different, and they are all delicious.

Prove It

What details explain why fruits and vegetables are categorized by color in this article?

Retell "Plants Are Alive!"

 To retell a selection about experiments, give the main steps (causes) and the outcomes (effects). You can use words such as *because* and *as a result*.

"Plants Are Alive!" is a procedural selection. Review the selection on pages 350–359. Look at each cause and effect on page 375.

■ First Cause and Effect: What happens when a plant's roots get no water?

■ Second Cause and Effect: What happens when a plant's leaves get no light?

■ Third Cause and Effect: What happens when a plant's stem is placed in colored water?

■ Conclusion: What do all the experiments tell us about plant parts?

Use the pictures on page 375 to retell the selection to your partner. As you give each cause and effect, point to the correct picture. Use complete sentences.

Words you might use in your retelling:		
photosynthesis	chlorophyll	nutrients
characteristic	complex	fluid

Cause

Effect

no water to roots

wilted and dry

no sunlight

pale patches

colored water

colored flower

Dig Deeper

Look Back

Look at all the diagrams and other graphic features in this unit. Use them to answer these questions on a sheet of paper.

1. What two main topics do the diagrams give information about?

2. What is one detail shown in a diagram that is not also in the text?

3. How do the diagrams of the experiments help explain how to do the experiments?

Talk About It

Imagine you saw a beautiful plant. How would you describe it?

> I saw a beautiful plant.
> It was right across the street from the school.

> The plant had purple petals.
> It smelled very sweet.

> I saw a beautiful plant right across the street from the school. The plant had purple petals and smelled very sweet.

Work with classmates. Come up with sentences that describe plants, trees, or flowers you have seen. Try combining the sentences in ways that make sense.

Conversation

 Sometimes you need to warn someone about something that is dangerous or unhealthy. If there is time, you can explain why something isn't good to do. If it is an emergency, warn the person with just one or two words.

Talk to a partner. One of you will be person A. The other will be person B.

Person A

Warn your partner of an emergency.

Warn your partner about something else. It is not an emergency.

Thank your partner.

Person B

Thank your partner.

Reply. Then warn your partner of an emergency.

Warn your partner about something else. It is not an emergency.

GLOSSARY

astronomy

A

am·pli·fy (ăm′plə-fī′) *v.* to make a sound louder or stronger

as·tron·o·my (ə-strŏn′ə-mē) *n.* the study of the stars and planets

ax·is (ăk′sĭs) *n.* an imaginary line that goes through the middle of Earth from the North Pole to the South Pole

B

bac·te·ri·a (băk-tîr′ē-ə) *n.pl.* some of the smallest living things

bat·tle (băt′l) *n.* a fight between groups of people

beat (bēt) *v.* the time and pattern of music

beat

bill (bĭl) *n.* a written draft for a new law

Bos·ton Tea Par·ty (bŏs′tən) (tē) (pär′tē) *n.* an event that happened in 1773 when American colonists protested a tax on tea by throwing the tea into Boston Harbor

ă pat / ā pay / âr care / ä father / ĕ pet / ē bee /
ĭ pit / ī pie / îr pier / ŏ pot / ō toe / ô paw /

brass in·stru·ments (brăs) (ĭn′strə-mənts)
n.pl instruments made of metal that make sound
when you blow through them

Brit·ish (brĭt′ĭsh) *adj.* describing the people
and things that come from Great Britain

C

camp (kămp) *n.* an outdoor area where people
can eat and sleep

brass instruments

car·a·van (kăr′ə-văn′) *n.* a group of people
who travel together on a challenging trip

char·ac·ter·is·tic (kăr′ək-tə-rĭs′tĭk) *n.* a
special feature or quality of a thing or person

checks and bal·anc·es (chĕks) (ănd)
(băl′əns-es) *n.pl.* a system where each branch of
government has the same amount of power as
the others

chlo·ro·phyll (klôr′ə-fĭl) *n.* the chemical that
makes leaves green

communicate

col·o·ny (kŏl′ə-nē) *n.* a group of people who
settle in a new land to live and work together

com·mu·ni·cate (kə-myoo′nĭ-kāt′) *v.* to
share your ideas, thoughts, or feelings with
someone else

oi **noise** / oͦo **took** / oō **boot** / ou **out** / ŭ **cut** / ûr **firm** / hw **which** /
th **thin** / *th* **this** / zh **vision** / ə **about, item, edible, gallop, circus**

com·plex (kəm-plĕks′) *adj.* having many parts

Con·gress (kŏng′grĭs) *n.* a group of people who are elected from each state and whose job is to propose and pass laws

con·sti·tu·tion (kŏn′stĭ-tōō′shən) *n.* the written document of a government's laws or rules

coordinate

con·tract (kən′trăkt′) *v.* to become smaller or shorter

co·op·er·ate (kō-ŏp′ə-rāt′) *intr.v.* to work together with someone

co·or·di·nate (kō-ôr′dn-āt′) *intr.v.* to make things work together

cor·al (kôr′əl) *n.* a stony material formed from the bones of small sea animals

cra·ter (krā′tər) *n.* a bowl-shaped hole in the ground caused by something big crashing

coral

D

de·clare (dĭ-klâr′) *v.* to say something out loud in front of others

de·moc·ra·cy (dĭ-mŏk′rə-sē) *n.* a type of government where people can speak and vote freely about what the government should do

ă pat / ā pay / âr care / ä father / ĕ pet / ē bee /
ĭ pit / ī pie / îr pier / ŏ pot / ō toe / ô paw /

de·pend (dĭ-pĕnd′) *intr.v.* to rely on or to need something from

depth (dĕpth) *n.* the distance from the top to the bottom of something

de·tect (dĭ-tĕkt′) *v.* to notice something that is not easy to see or hear

de·vel·op (dĭ-vĕl′əp) *v.* to think of a new idea, or to produce a new product

de·vice (dĭ-vīs′) *n.* a tool that is made to do a special job

dis·tance (dĭs′təns) *n.* the amount of space between two places or things

doc·u·ment (dŏk′yə-mənt) *n.* an official paper

E

ear·drum (îr′drŭm′) *n.* the thin layer of skin between the outer ear and the inner ear

ech·o (ĕk′ō) *n.* a sound made when sound waves bounce off something and make it seem as if the sound is repeated

e·mo·tion (ĭ-mō′shən) *n.* a strong feeling such as happiness or sadness

detect

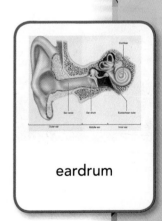

eardrum

oi n**oi**se / ŏŏ t**oo**k / ōō b**oo**t / ou **ou**t / ŭ c**u**t / ûr f**ir**m / hw **wh**ich /
th **th**in / *th* **th**is / zh vi**s**ion / ə **a**bout, **i**tem, ed**i**ble, gall**o**p, circ**u**s

en·vi·ron·ment (ĕn-vī′rən-mənt) *n.* all the things that surround people, animals, and plants as they live

e·quip·ment (ĭ-kwĭp′mənt) *n.* things needed or used for a certain purpose

equipment

ex·ec·u·tive branch (ĭg-zĕk′yə-tĭv) (brănch) *n.* the part of the government that is responsible for enforcing laws and protecting the country

ex·ist (ĭg-zĭst′) *intr.v.* to be real or alive

ex·pe·di·tion (ĕk′spĭ-dĭsh′ən) *n.* a long trip that has a purpose

ex·plo·sion (ĭk-splō′zhən) *n.* the breaking apart of something with a lot of force and noise

F

flight (flīt) *n.* a trip in air or space

flu·id (floo′ĭd) *n.* a liquid

flight

fron·tier (frŭn-tîr′) *n.* the open land beyond all settled areas

G

gov·ern (gŭv′ərn) *v.* to rule over a place and help make laws for the people who live there

ă pat / ā pay / âr care / ä father / ĕ pet / ē bee /
ĭ pit / ī pie / îr pier / ŏ pot / ō toe / ô paw /

gov·ern·ment (gŭv′ərn-mənt) *n.* a group of people in charge of a city, state, or country

guide (gīd) *n.* a person who shows people a new place and gives them information about the place

H

hard·ship (härd′shĭp′) *n.* something that causes problems or challenges

hardship

his·tor·ic (hĭ-stôr′ĭk) *adj.* important in history

I

im·pact (ĭm′păkt′) *n.* the powerful effect something has on someone or something else

im·prove (ĭm-prōōv′) *v.* to make something better than it was before

in·de·pen·dence (ĭn′dĭ-pĕn′dəns) *n.* the ability to act freely, without being told what to do

impact

in·ner plan·ets (ĭn′ər) (plăn′ĭts) *n.pl.* the four planets closest to the Sun: Mercury, Venus, Earth, and Mars

in·no·va·tion (ĭn′ə-vā′shən) *n.* a new idea, a new invention, or a new way of doing something

oi noise / ŏŏ took / ōō boot / ou out / ŭ cut / ûr firm / hw which / th thin / *th* this / zh vision / ə about, item, edible, gallop, circus

in·ter·pret (ĭn-tûr′prĭt) *v.* to decide what something means

in·ven·tion (ĭn-věn′shən) *n.* something that is made for the first time

in·vol·un·tar·y (ĭn-vŏl′ən-tĕr′ē) *adj.* done without control, choice, or will

justice

J

jour·ney (jûr′nē) *n.* a long trip from one place to another

ju·di·cial branch (jōō-dĭsh′əl) (brănch) *n.* the part of the government that decides if laws are fair

jus·tice (jŭs′tĭs) *n.* fair treatment under the law

L

launch

la·bor (lā′bər) *n.* work, especially work that needs a lot of physical effort and strength

launch (lônch) *v.* to fly into space

leg·is·la·tive branch (lĕj′ĭ-slā′tĭv) (brănch) *n.* the part of the government that writes and passes new laws

lib·er·ty (lĭb′ər-tē) *n.* the freedom to live as we want

ă pat / ā pay / âr care / ä father / ě pet / ē bee /
ĭ pit / ī pie / îr pier / ŏ pot / ō toe / ô paw /

life form (līf) (fôrm) *n.* a living thing such as a plant or animal

lu·nar (lo͞o′nər) *adj.* relating to the Moon

M

march (märch) *n.* the act of walking together in a group for a reason

ma·rine (mə-rēn′) *adj.* relating to things that live in the ocean

marine

med·i·cine (měd′ĭ-sĭn) *n.* the study of how to treat diseases and injuries of the body

mis·sion (mĭsh′ən) *n.* a church

mod·el (mŏd′l) *n.* a small copy of something

muf·fle (mŭf′əl) *tr.v.* to make a sound quieter

N

net·work (nět′wûrk′) *n.* a group of parts that are connected

network

nerves (nûrvs) *n.pl.* string-like fibers that connect the brain and spinal cord to other parts of the body, and carry messages to and from the brain

note (nōt) *n.* a single sound on the musical scale

oi noise / o͝o took / o͞o boot / ou out / ŭ cut / ûr firm / hw which / th thin / *th* this / zh vision / ə about, item, edible, gallop, circus

nu·tri·ents (nōō′trē-ənts) *n.pl.* the materials in food that provide energy to plants and animals

O

online

on·line (ŏn′līn′) *adj.* connected to the Internet, or to other computers through the Internet

or·gan·ism (ôr′gə-nĭz′əm) *n.* any living thing

out·er plan·ets (ou′tər) (plăn′ĭts) *n.pl.* the four planets farthest from the Sun: Jupiter, Saturn, Uranus, and Neptune

ox·y·gen (ŏk′sĭ-jən) *n.* a gas in the air we breathe that has no color, smell, or taste

P

pam·phlet (păm′flĭt) *n.* a thin booklet that explains ideas or information in a few pages

pat·ent (păt′nt) *n.* an official government document that gives the right to be the only person to make, use, or sell an invention

per·cus·sion in·stru·ments (pər-kŭsh′ən) (ĭn′strə-mənts) *n.pl.* instruments that make a sound when shaken or struck with a stick

photosynthesis

pho·to·syn·the·sis (fō′tō-sĭn′thĭ-sĭs) *n.* the way that green plants make their food

pi·o·neer (pī′ə-nîr′) *n.* one of the first people to settle a place

ă pat / ā pay / âr care / ä father / ĕ pet / ē bee /
ĭ pit / ī pie / îr pier / ŏ pot / ō toe / ô paw /

pitch (pĭch) *n.* the high or low quality of a sound

po·lit·i·cal par·ty (pə-lĭt′ĭ-kəl) (pär′tē) *n.* a group of people who share ideas about how government should work

prop·er·ty (prŏp′ər-tē) *n.* things that are owned

pro·test (prə-tĕst′) *v.* to join with others to show strong disagreement with something

protest

pulse (pŭls) *n.* the regular beat of blood as it is pumped through the body by the heart

R

rate (rāt) *n.* the number of times something happens during a period of time

re·flect (rĭ-flĕkt′) *v.* to bounce back from a surface

re·fuse (rĭ-fyōōz′) *v.* to say you will not do something

rep·re·sent (rĕp′rĭ-zĕnt′) *tr.v.* to stand up for the rights and interests of others

reflect

res·pi·ra·tion (rĕs′pə-rā′shən) *n.* the process of breathing in and out

rev·o·lu·tion (rĕv′ə-lōō′shən) *n.* when people fight to change their country's government

oi noise / ŏŏ took / ōō boot / ou out / ŭ cut / ûr firm / hw which / th thin / *th* this / zh vision / ə about, item, edible, gallop, circus

re·volve (rǐ-vǒlv′) *v.* to move around a central point

rights (rīts) *n.* the things we can do by law

rov·er (rō′vər) *n.* a robot that scientists send to travel on the surface of the Moon or a planet to collect information

satellite

S

salt wa·ter (sôlt) (wô′tər) *n.* water that has salt in it

sat·el·lite (sǎt′l-īt′) *n.* a manufactured object that is sent into space to move around Earth and send information from one place to another

sea·weed (sē′wēd′) *n.* any plant that grows in the ocean

sound waves (sound) (wāvs) *n.pl.* vibrations that travel through the air

space·craft (spās′krǎft′) *n.* a vehicle that flies and travels in space

steamboat

space sta·tion (spās) (stā′shən) *n.* a structure in space where people live and work

stage·coach (stāj′kōch′) *n.* a large, closed wagon with four wheels that is pulled by horses

steam·boat (stēm′bōt′) *n.* a boat that is powered by a steam engine

ă pat / ā pay / âr care / ä father / ĕ pet / ē bee / ǐ pit / ī pie / îr pier / ŏ pot / ō toe / ô paw /

string in·stru·ments (strĭng) (ĭn′strə-mənts) *n.pl.* instruments that make sound when you play the strings with your hands or with a bow

Su·preme Court (soõ-prēm′) (kôrt) *n.* the highest court of the United States

sur·face (sûr′fəs) *n.* the outside or the top of something

sur·round (sə-round′) *tr.v.* something that is all around you

sur·vive (sər-vīv′) *v.* to stay alive even if it is difficult

string instruments

T

tech·nol·o·gy (tĕk-nŏl′ə-jē) *n.* new machines and new inventions that people make by using their knowledge of science

tel·e·graph (tĕl′ĭ-grăf′) *n.* a machine that sends electrical messages over wires

tel·e·scope (tĕl′ĭ-skōp′) *n.* a tool you can use to look at objects that are very far away

transparent

trans·par·ent (trăns-pâr′ənt) *adj.* clear and able to be seen through

trench (trĕnch) *n.* a long, narrow ditch

troops (troõps) *n.pl.* soldiers

oi **noise** / oo **took** / ōo **boot** / ou **out** / ŭ **cut** / ûr **firm** / hw **which** / th **thin** / *th* **this** / zh **vision** / ə **about, item, edible, gallop, circus**

V

ve·to (vē′tō) *v.* when a person says no to an idea

volume

vi·bra·tion (vī-brā′shən) *n.* what happens when something moves up and down or back and forth very quickly

vol·ume (vŏl′yo͞om) *n.* the amount of sound made by a musical instrument, voice, radio, TV, or CD player

vol·un·tar·y (vŏl′ən-tĕr′ē) *adj.* done by choice

W

wag·on (wăg′ən) *n.* a vehicle with four wheels, pulled by horses, and used for carrying heavy loads

westward expansion

west·ward ex·pan·sion (wĕst′wərd) (ĭk-spăn′shən) *n.* what happened when settlers moved to new lands west of the Mississippi River

wind in·stru·ments (wĭnd) (ĭn′strə-mənts) *n.pl.* instruments that make sound when you blow through them and use certain finger patterns to cover the holes

Z

zone (zōn) *n.* an area or part of something

ă pat / ā pay / âr care / ä father / ĕ pet / ē bee /
ĭ pit / ī pie / îr pier / ŏ pot / ō toe / ô paw /

Acknowledgments

Text Acknowledgments: "the drum" from *Spin a Soft Black Song, Revised Edition* by Nikki Giovanni. Text copyright © 1971 by Nikki Giovanni. Reprinted by permission of Farrar, Straus & Giroux, LLC.

Excerpt from *Early Thunder* by Jean Fritz. Text copyright © 1967 by Jean Fritz. Reprinted by permission of Puffin Books, a division of Penguin Group (USA) Inc. and the Gina Maccoby Literary Agency.

"Skyscraper" from *We the People: Poems* by Bobbi Katz. Text copyright © 1998, 2000 by Bobbi Katz. Reprinted by permission of HarperCollins Publishers.

"This Is Just to Say" from *The Collected Poems: Volume I*, 1909-1939 by William Carlos Williams. Text copyright © 1938 by the New Directions Publishing Corp. Reprinted by permission of New Directions Publishing Corp. and Carcanet.

Illustration Credits: Margaret Kasahara; Vitali Konstantinov; Jonny Mendelsson; Ed Parker; Kyle Still; Susan Swan; Franklin Hammond; Tony Klassen; Chris Lensch; Kevin Rechin; Elizabeth Sayles; Darryl Shelton; Lisa Adams; Richard Downs; Trevor Howard; Christopher Corr; Linda Holt-Ayress; Darryl Ligasan; Patrice Rossi-Calkin; John Sandford; Gerardo Suzan; John Sandford; Stacey Schuett; Neil Shigley; Joel Spector; Tim Jessell; David A. Jonason; Jason O'Malley; Kris Wiltse; Karen Blessen; Patrick Corrigan; David A. Jonason; Kim and James Neale, Studio Promotions; Sam Ward; Darryl Ligasan; Kate Sweeney; Teresa Villegas, Nicole Wong, Escletxa.

Photography Credits: iv (t) ©Houghton Mifflin Harcourt; iv ©Joe Sohm/Visions of America/Getty Images; iv (br) © NASA; v (t) Photodisc/Getty Images; v © Courtesy of Texas Highways Magazine (Tx Dot); v ©Getty Images; vi (t) ©Avraham/Fotolia; vi ©Photodisc/ Getty Royalty Free; vii (bl) ©Digital Vision/Getty Images; vii Brand X Pictures/Getty Images; vii ©C Squared Studios/Photodisc/Getty Images; vii © Getty Images; ix © Artville / Getty Images; ix (b) Michael Saul/Brand X/Corbis; ix Getty Images/Photodisc; 2 (c) ©Hulton Fine Art Collection/Getty Images; 2 (c) ©Stockbyte/Getty Images; 2 (b) Hisham F. Ibrahim/Photodisc/Getty Images; 3 (b) ©Digital Vision/Getty Images; 3 Corbis; 3 © Getty Images; 3 (t) © Getty Images; 4 (t) © Varijanta/Shutterstock; 4 (br) Photodisc/Getty Images; 4 Getty Images/Photodisc; 4 ©Getty Images; 5 © NASA; 5 (t) © NASA; 6 (b) © Comstock/ Getty Images RF; 7 Superstock, Inc/Superstock; 8 Stockbyte/Getty Images; 8 (t) © Corbis Royalty Free; 9 (br) ©BIG CHEESE PHOTO LLC SPECIAL/Alamy; 9 (cr) © Hisham Ibrahim/Photodisc/ Getty Images; 9 (tr) ©Joe Sohm/Visions of America/Getty Images; 18 (c) ©Tobias Helbig/Getty Images; 18 (l) Getty Images/ Photodisc; 19 (r) Getty Images/Photodisc; 22 (b) © Comstock/ Getty Images RF; 23 (b) Comstock/ Getty Images; 24 (bg) Liquidlibrary/Jupiterimages/Getty Images; 24 (c) ©Stock Montage/Archive Photos/Getty Images; 25 (c) ©Stockbyte/Getty Images; 25 (c) ©Hulton Fine Art Collection/Getty Images; 26 ©Roel Smart/Getty Images; 27 Stockbyte / Getty Images; 27 (b) ©Eris Isselee/Shutterstock; 28 ©Roel Smart/Getty Images; 28 (b) ©FotografiaBasica/Getty Images; 29 Stockbyte / Getty Images; 29 (bl) ©Richard Goerg/Getty Images; 30 ©Roel Smart/Getty Images; 30 (br) ©NiKreationS/Alamy; 30 (bl) ©Denis Jr. Tangney/Getty Images; 31 Stockbyte / Getty Images; 31 (tr) ©Patrick Strattner/Getty Images; 32 ©Roel Smart/Getty Images; 33 Stockbyte / Getty Images; 34 ©Roel Smart/Getty Images; 34 (tr) ©Denis Jr. Tangney/Getty Images; 35 Stockbyte / Getty Images; 35 (b) ©Robert Whitworth/Getty Images; 45 (t) Photodisc/Getty Images; 52 ©Brand X Pictures/ Age Fotostock; 52 (bl) © Bettmann/CORBIS; 52 © Scott J. Ferrell/Congressional Quarterly/Getty Images; 54 (bl) Hisham F. Ibrahim/Photodisc/Getty Images; 54 © Alamy Images Royalty Free; 54 © Andersen Ross/Blend/Getty Images; 54 (br) © Eyewire/Getty Images Royalty Free; 55 © Getty Images Royalty Free; 64 (tl) Photodisc/Getty Images; 64 (bc) Jupiterim-ages/Getty Images; 65 (br) Comstock/Getty Images; 66 (br) © White House Collection, photographer Eric Draper; 66 (cl) © United States Mint; 66 (b) ©Getty Images; 67 (cr) © John F. Kennedy Library; 67 © David J. & Janice L. Frent Collection/ CORBIS; 67 (tl) Bettmann/Corbis; 68 (cl) © White House Collection, photographer Pete Souza; 68 (br) © Ronald Reagan Library; 68 (tr) © Bettmann/Corbis; 68 (cr) © Joseph Sohm/Visions of America/Corbis; 69 (tl) © Franklin Delano Roosevelt Library; 69 Library of Congress; 69 ©Bettmann/CORBIS; 69 (bl) ©Museum of the City of New York/Corbis; 70 (bl) © John Henley/Corbis; 70 (tl) © Paul Barton/Corbis; 71 (bg) © Joseph Sohm/Corbis; 72 (bg) ©Robin2/Shutterstock; 72 (c) © Brand X Pictures/Jupiterimages Corporation; 74 (bg) ©Robin2/Shutterstock; 78 ©Brand X/AGE fotostock; 79 Getty Images/ Digital Vision; 80 Getty Images/PhotoDisc; 81 (t) Creatas/Jupiterimages/Getty Images; 82 (l) Stockdisc/Getty Images; 82 (cl) ©Comstock Images/Getty Images; 82 (bl) ©Corbis; 83 (tr) Dynamic Graphics/Jupiterimages/Getty Images; 83 (tr) Chris Ryan/Getty Images; 84 (tl) Photodisc/Getty Images; 84 (bl) ©Comstock/Getty Images; 84 (b) ©Radius Images/Alamy; 84 (bl) Getty Images/PhotoDisc; 85 (tr) Artville/Getty Images; 85 (tr) ©HBSS/Age Fotostock; 85 (tr) ©Corbis; 85 (br) Stockdisc/ Getty Images; 86 (bl) Jupiterimages/Getty Images; 86 (tr) © PhotoDisc/Getty Images; 87 (br) Artville/Getty Images; 87 (b) ©Corbis; 87 (b) Stockdisc/Getty Images; 87 (b) ©Royalty-Free/ CORBIS; 87 (b) © Corbis RF; 87 (b) ©Corbis; 90 (bc) Getty Images; 92 ©Joseph Sohm-Visions of America/Digital Vision/Getty Images; 93 (t) ©Fotolia; 93 (c) © Corbis; 93 (c) ©Spirit of America/Shutterstock; 95 ©Brand X/AGE fotostock; 95 (c) Getty Images/Digital Vision; 95 (cr) Getty Images/PhotoDisc; 95 (br) © Collection of the Supreme Court of the United States; 95 (bc) © White House Collection, photographer Pete Souza; 95 (bl) © Scott J. Ferrell/Congressional Quarterly/Getty Images; 97 (br) Blend Images/Alamy; 98 ©DLILLC/Corbis; 98 © Getty Images; 99 ©Thinkstock/Alamy Images; 100 (cl) © Getty Images; 100 (c) © Getty Images; 101 (br) © Corbis Royalty Free; 101 (c) ©Getty Images; 101 © Artville / Getty Images; 101 (tr) © Getty Images; 108 (tr) © Stockdisk / Getty Images; 108 Stockbyte/Getty Images; 108 Photodisc/Getty Images; 108 (tl) © Getty Images; 108 ©Getty Images; 108 © Artville / Getty Images; 109 © C Squared Studios/PhotoDisc/ Getty Images; 109 © Getty Images; 109 (br) © C Squared Studios/ PhotoDisc/ Getty Images; 109 © Artville / Getty Images; 109 (bl) © Jupiter Unlimited Royalty Free; 110 (tc) Dynamic Graphics/Jupiterimages/Getty Images; 110 (tl) Creatas / Getty Images; 110 (bl) © Photos.com/Jupiterimages Corporation; 110 (bl) ©rangizzz/Shutterstock; 111 (bl) Creatas / Getty Images; 111 (br) Comstock/Getty Images; 112 (tr) © PhotoDisc/ Getty Images; 112 (cr) © Getty Images; 113 (cl) © Corbis Royalty Free; 113 (cl) © AFP/Getty Images; 113 (tr) ©PhotoDisc/ Getty Images; 114 (tr) Artville/Getty Images; 114 (tl) © C Squared Studios/PhotoDisc/ Getty Images; 114 (bl) ©Wu Wei/ XinHua/Xinhua; 115 (bl) © C Squared Studios/PhotoDisc/Getty Images; 115 (cr) © PhotoSpin, Inc./ Alamy; 115 (br) © C Squared Studios/PhotoDisc/ Getty Images; 115 (tc) © Reuters NewsMedia/Corbis; 116 (r) ©Getty Images; 117 (tr) ©Creatas/Getty Images; 117 (tr) ©Creatas/Getty Images; 117 (b) Creatas / Getty Images; 117 (b) ©PhotoDisc/Getty Images; 124 (tl) ©Naoki Okamoto/Photodisc/Getty Images; 124 (tr) ©Dmitry Pichugin/Fotolia; 124 (br) © Corbis; 125 (tr) ©Corbis; 125 (tr) ©Redferns/Getty Images; 125 (b) Getty Images; 126 (tl) Corbis; 126 (b) ©Image Source/Getty Images; 127 (t) ©Don Farrall/Photodisc/Getty Images; 127 (tr) Photodisc/Getty Images; 127 (tr) ©Corbis; 127 (tr) ©Corbis; 136 (t)